GOD'S PROMISES FOR YOUR LIFE

GOD'S PROMISES FOR YOUR LIFE

-Elizabeth Tupou-

APRress
45 Dan Road Suite 5
Canton MA 02021

Hotline: 1(888) 821-0229
Fax: 1(508) 545-7580

Ordering Information:
Quantity sales. Special discounts are available on quantity purchases by corporations, associations, and others. For details, contact the publisher at the address above.

ISBN-13:   Paperback   979-8-89356-875-2
                  eBook   979-8-89356-876-9

Library of Congress Control Number: 2024909126

DEDICATION

This book is dedicated to my sister Helen whose kindness, forgiveness and open heart to everyone, has always displayed the body of the gospel and been a constant assurance that God's love is real, even during times when He seems far away.

Contents

THE BIBLE IS THE WORD OF GOD AND OUR GUIDE FOR EVERY DAY

Matthew 24:35 Heaven and earth will pass away, but my words will not pass away.

John 1:1 In the beginning was the Word, and the Word was with God, and the Word was God.

2 Timothy 3:16-17 All Scripture is breathed out by God and profitable for teaching, for reproof, for correction, and for training in righteousness, that the man of God may be competent, equipped for every good work.

Isaiah 40:8 The grass withers, the flower fades, but the word of our God will stand forever.

Isaiah 55:11 So shall my word be that goes out from my mouth; it shall not return to me empty, but it shall accomplish that which I purpose, and shall succeed in the thing for which I sent it.

Psalm 119:160 The sum of your word is truth, and every one of your righteous rules endures forever.

Psalm 119:105 Your word is[a] a lamp for my feet, a light for my pathway.

Psalm 119:11 I have stored what you have said[a] in my heart, so I won't sin against you.

Deuteronomy 6:5-9 [5] You are to love the Lord your God with all your heart, all your soul, and all your strength. [6] Let these words that I'm commanding you today be always[a] on your heart. [7] Teach them repeatedly to your children. Talk about them while sitting in your house or walking on the road, and as you lie down or get up. [8] Tie them as reminders[b] on your forearm, bind them on your forehead,[c] [9] and write them on the door frames of your house and on your gates."

John 8:31-32 [31] So Jesus told those Jews who had believed in him, "If you continue in my word, you are really my disciples. [32] And you will know the truth, and the truth will set you free."

2 Timothy 3:16-17 [16] All Scripture is God-breathed[a] and is useful for teaching, for reproof, for correction, and for training in righteousness, [17] so that the man of God may be complete, thoroughly equipped for every good action.

THE BIBLE: THE FINAL AUTHORITY

2 Timothy 3:16-17 [16] All Scripture is inspired by God and is useful for teaching, for showing people what is wrong in their lives, for correcting faults, and for teaching how to live right. [17] Using the Scriptures, the person who serves God will be capable, having all that is needed to do every good work.

2 Peter 1:20-21 [20] Most of all, you must understand this: No prophecy in the Scriptures ever comes from the prophet's own interpretation. [21] No prophecy ever came from what a person wanted to say, but people led by the Holy Spirit spoke words from God.

Hebrews 4:12-13 [12] God's word is alive and working and is sharper than a double-edged sword. It cuts all the way into us, where the soul and the spirit are joined, to the center of our joints and bones. And it judges the thoughts and feelings in our hearts. [13] Nothing in all the world can be hidden from God. Everything is clear and lies open before him, and to him we must explain the way we have lived.

Isaiah 55:10-11 For as the rain and the snow come down from heaven, And do not return there without watering the earth And making it produce and sprout, And providing seed to the sower and bread to the eater; [11] So will My word be which goes out of My mouth; It will not return to Me empty, Without accomplishing what I desire, And without succeeding *in the purpose* for which I sent it.

Mark 13:31 [31] Heaven and earth will pass away, but My words will not pass away.

Ephesians 6:17 And take the helmet of salvation and the sword of the Spirit, which is the word of God.

1 Peter 1:23-25 [23] for you have been born again not of seed which is perishable, but imperishable, that is, through the living and enduring word of God. [24] For, "All flesh is like grass, And all its glory is like the flower of grass. The grass withers, And the flower falls off, [25] But the word of the Lord endures forever." And this is the word which was [a]preached to you.

Psalm 33:8-9 Let all the earth fear the Lord; Let all the inhabitants of the world stand in awe of Him. [9] For He spoke, and it was done; He commanded, and it [a]stood firm.

Proverbs 30:5 Every word of God is [a]pure; He is a shield to those who take refuge in Him.

Psalm 119:89 Forever, Lord, Your word stands in heaven.

THE BIBLE
IS YOUR GUIDE FOR LIFE

Psalm 119:105 Your word is a lamp to my feet And a light to my path.

Proverbs 6:20-23 My son, comply with the commandment of your father, And do not ignore the [a]teaching of your mother; 21 Bind them continually on your heart; Tie them around your neck. 22 When you walk, [b]they will guide you; When you sleep, [c]they will watch over you; And when you awake, [d]they will talk to you. 23 For the commandment is a lamp and the [e]teaching is light; And rebukes for discipline are the way of life.

Psalm 119:11 I have treasured Your word in my heart, so that I may not sin against You.

Psalm 19:8-11 The precepts of the Lord are right, rejoicing the heart; The commandment of the Lord is pure, enlightening the eyes. 9 The fear of the Lord is clean, enduring forever; The judgments of the Lord are true; they are righteous altogether. 10 They are more desirable than gold, yes, than much pure gold, Sweeter also than honey and drippings of the honeycomb. 11 Moreover, Your servant is warned by them; In keeping them there is great reward.

Psalm 119:9 How can a young man keep his way pure?
By keeping *it* according to Your word.

John 8:31-32 31 So Jesus was saying to those Jews who had believed Him, "If you continue in My word, *then* you are truly My disciples; 32 and you will know the truth, and the truth will set you free."

2 Timothy 3:16-17 16 All Scripture is [a]inspired by God and beneficial for teaching, for [b]rebuke, for correction, for training in righteousness; 17 so that the man or woman of God may be [c]fully capable, equipped for every good work.

Psalm 119:24 Thy testimonies also are my delight and my counsellors.

2 Peter 1:4 [4] Through these he gave us the very great and precious promises. With these gifts you can share in God's nature, and the world will not ruin you with its evil desires.

Psalm 37:23-24 When people's steps follow the Lord, God is pleased with their ways. [24] If they stumble, they will not fall, because the Lord holds their hand.

Psalm 32:8 The Lord says, "I will make you wise and show you where to go. I will guide you and watch over you.

Psalm 23:3 He restores my soul; He guides me in the paths of righteousness For His name's sake.

Isaiah 30:21 [21] Your ears will hear a word behind you, saying, "This is the way, walk in it," whenever you turn to the right or to the left.

Joshua 1:8 [8] This Book of the Law shall not depart from your mouth, but you shall meditate on it day and night, so that you may be careful to do according to all that is written in it; for then you will make your way prosperous, and then you will achieve success.

THE BIBLE
IS YOUR SOLID ROCK

1 Peter 1:23-25 [23] for you have been born again not of seed which is perishable, but imperishable, *that is*, through the living and enduring word of God. [24] For, "All flesh is like grass, And all its glory is like the flower of grass. The grass withers, And the flower falls off, [25] But the word of the Lord endures forever."

And this is the word which was [a]preached to you.

Matthew 24:35 [35] Heaven and earth will pass away, but My words will not pass away.

Psalm 119:89 Forever, Lord, Your word stands in heaven.

Matthew 5:18 [18] For truly I say to you, until heaven and earth pass away, not [a]the smallest letter or stroke of a letter shall pass from the Law, until all is accomplished!

1 Kings 8:56 [56] "Blessed be the Lord, who has given rest to His people Israel in accordance with everything that He [a]promised; not one word has [b]failed of all His good [c]promise, which He [d]promised through Moses His servant.

Jude 24-25 [24] Now to Him who is able to protect you from stumbling, and to make you stand in the presence of His glory, blameless with great joy, [25] to the only God our Savior, through Jesus Christ our Lord, *be* glory, majesty, dominion, and authority before all time and now and [a]forever. Amen.

Ezekiel 12:24-25 [24] For there will no longer be any [a]false vision or deceptive divination within the house of Israel. [25] For I the Lord will speak whatever word I speak, and it will be performed. It will no longer be delayed, for in your days, you rebellious house, I will speak the word and perform it," declares the Lord God.'"

Proverbs 4:20-22 [20] My son, pay attention to my words; Incline your ear to my sayings. [21] They are not to escape from your sight; Keep them in the midst of your heart. [22] For they are life to those who find them, And healing to all [a]their body.

Psalm 40:2-3 He brought me up out of the pit of [a]destruction, out of the mud; And He set my feet on a rock, making my footsteps firm. [3] He put a new song in my mouth, a song of praise to our God; Many will see and fear And will trust in the Lord.

THE BIBLE ENCOURAGES US TO TAKE GOD AS OUR SOURCE OF STRENTH

Philippians 4:13 I can do all things through him who strengthens me.

Isaiah 41:10 Fear not, for I am with you; be not dismayed, for I am your God; I will strengthen you, I will help you, I will uphold you with my righteous right hand.

Isaiah 40:31 But they who wait for the Lord shall renew their strength; they shall mount up with wings like eagles; they shall run and not be weary; they shall walk and not faint.

Exodus 15:2 The Lord is my strength and my song, and he has become my salvation; this is my God, and I will praise him, my father's God, and I will exalt him.

Ephesians 6:10 Finally, be strong in the Lord and in the strength of his might.

Deuteronomy 31:6 Be strong and courageous. Do not be afraid or terrified because of them, for the Lord your God goes with you; he will never leave you nor forsake you.

Exodus 15:2 The Lord is my strength and my defense; he has become my salvation. He is my God, and I will praise him, my father's God, and I will exalt him.

1 Chronicles 16:11 Look to the Lord and his strength; seek his face always.

Joshua 1:9 Have I not commanded you? Be strong and courageous. Do not be afraid; do not be discouraged, for the Lord your God will be with you wherever you go."

2 Timothy 1:7 For the Spirit God gave us does not make us timid, but gives us power, love and self-discipline.

Matthew 11:28 Come to me, all you who are weary and burdened, and I will give you rest.

Habakkuk 3:19 The Sovereign Lord is my strength; he makes my feet like the feet of a deer; he enables me to tread on the heights.

Psalm 118:14 The Lord is my strength and my defense; he has become my salvation.

Psalm 28:7-8 The Lord is my strength and my shield; my heart trusts in him, and he helps me. My heart leaps for joy, and with my song I praise him. [8] The Lord is the strength of his people, a fortress of salvation for his anointed one.

1 Corinthians 16:13 Be on your guard; stand firm in the faith; be courageous; be strong.

Daniel 10:19 Do not be afraid, you who are highly esteemed," he said. "Peace! Be strong now; be strong." When he spoke to me, I was strengthened and said, "Speak, my lord, since you have given me strength.

Psalm 46:1-3 God is our refuge and strength, an ever-present help in trouble. [2] Therefore we will not fear, though the earth gives way and the mountains fall into the heart of the sea, [3] though its waters roar and foam and the mountains quake with their surging.

Proverbs 18:10 The name of the Lord is a fortified tower; the righteous run to it and are safe.

Psalm 32:7-8 You are my hiding place; you will protect me from trouble and surround me with songs of deliverance. [8] I will instruct you and teach you in the way you should go; I will counsel you with my loving eye on you.

Deuteronomy 31:8 The Lord himself goes before you and will be with you; he will never leave you nor forsake you. Do not be afraid; do not be discouraged."

John 14:27 Peace I leave with you; my peace I give you. I do not give to you as the world gives. Do not let your hearts be troubled and do not be afraid.

Psalm 27:1-3 The Lord is my light and my salvation- whom shall I fear? The Lord is the stronghold of my life- of whom shall I be afraid? ²When the wicked advance against me to devour me, it is my enemies and my foes who will stumble and fall. ³Though an army besiege me, my heart will not fear; though war break out against me, even then I will be confident.

Psalm 16:8 I keep my eyes always on the Lord. With him at my right hand, I will not be shaken.

2 Corinthians 12:9 But he said to me, "My grace is sufficient for you, for my power is made perfect in weakness." Therefore, I will boast all the more gladly about my weaknesses, so that Christ's power may rest on me.

Ephesians 6:10 Finally, be strong in the Lord and in his mighty power.

1 Corinthians 10:13 No temptation has overtaken you except what is common to mankind. And God is faithful; he will not let you be tempted beyond what you can bear. But when you are tempted, he will also provide a way out so that you can endure it.

Isaiah 40:29 He gives strength to the weary and increases the power of the weak.

Psalm 73:26 My flesh and my heart may fail, but God is the strength of my heart and my portion forever.

Psalm 31:24 Be strong and take heart, all you who hope in the Lord.

2 Thessalonians 3:3 But the Lord is faithful, and he will strengthen you and protect you from the evil one.

2 Corinthians 12:10 That is why, for Christ's sake, I delight in weaknesses, in insults, in hardships, in persecutions, in difficulties. For when I am weak, then I am strong.

Psalm 18:32 It is God who arms me with strength and keeps my way secure.

2 Corinthians 4:16-17 Therefore we do not lose heart. Though outwardly we are wasting away, yet inwardly we are being renewed day by day. 17 For our light and momentary troubles are achieving for us an eternal glory that far outweighs them all.

JESUS: OUR SAVIOR AND OUR GOD

Titus 4:10 In grace our Savior God appeared, to make his love for mankind clear. [5] 'Twas not for deeds that we had done, but by his steadfast love alone he saved us through a second birth, renewed us by the Spirit's work, [6] and poured him out upon us, too, through Jesus the Messiah our Savior true. [7] And so, made heirs by his own grace, eternal life we now embrace.

Luke 19:9-10 [9] Then Jesus told him, "Today salvation has come to this home, because this man is also a descendant of Abraham, [10] and the Son of Man has come to seek and to save the lost."

John 3:16-17 [16] "For this is how God loved the world: He gave his uniquely existing Son so that everyone who believes in him would not be lost but have eternal life. [17] Because God sent the Son into the world, not t[9] If you declare with your mouth that Jesus is Lord and believe in your heart that God raised him from the dead, you will be saved not to condemn the world, but that the world would be saved through him.

Romans 10:9 [9] If you declare with your mouth that Jesus is Lord and believe in your heart that God raised him from the dead, you will be saved.

John 12:47 [47] If anyone hears my words and doesn't keep them, I don't condemn him, because I didn't come to condemn the world, but to save it.[a]

Ephesians 2:4-8 [4] But God, who is rich in mercy, because of his great love for us[a] [5] even when we were dead because of our offenses, made us alive together with[b] the Messiah[c] (by grace you have been saved), [6] raised us up with him, and seated us with him in the heavenly realm in the Messiah[d] Jesus, [7] so that in the coming ages he might display the limitless riches of his grace that comes to us through his kindness in the Messiah[e] Jesus. [8] For by such grace you have been saved through faith. This does not come from you; it is the gift of God.

2 Timothy 1:8-10 [8] Therefore, never be ashamed of the testimony about our Lord or of me, his prisoner. Instead, by God's power, join me in suffering for the sake of the gospel.

[9] He saved us and called us with a holy calling, not according to our own accomplishments, but according to his own purpose and the grace that was given to us in the Messiah[a] Jesus before time began.[b] [10] Now, however, that grace[c] has been revealed through the coming of our Savior the Messiah[d] Jesus, who has destroyed death and through the gospel has brought life and release from death into full view.

Psalm 106:8 He delivered for the sake of his name, to make his power known.

1 John 4:10 [10] This is love: not that we have loved[a] God, but that he loved us and sent his Son to be the atoning sacrifice for our sins.

JESUS:
IS HE YOUR LORD?

Philippians 2:9-11 Now lifted up by God to heaven, a name above all others given, this matchless name possessing. ¹⁰ And so, when Jesus' name is called, the knees of everyone should fall, wherever they're residing. ¹¹ Then every tongue in one accord, will say that Jesus the Messiah is Lord, while God the Father praising.

Matthew 4:10 Then Jesus said to him, "Be gone, Satan! For it is written, "'You shall worship the Lord your God and him only shall you serve.'"

John 4:16 Jesus said to him, "I am the way, and the truth, and the life. No one comes to the Father except through me.

John 20:28 Thomas answered him, "My Lord and my God!"

Romans 10:9-13 Because, if you confess with your mouth that Jesus is Lord and believe in your heart that God raised him from the dead, you will be saved. For with the heart one believes and is justified, and with the mouth one confesses and is saved. For the Scripture says, "Everyone who believes in him will not be put to shame." For there is no distinction between Jew and Greek; for the same Lord is Lord of all, bestowing his riches on all who call on him. For "everyone who calls on the name of the Lord will be saved."

1 Timothy 6:14-16   To keep the commandment unstained and free from reproach until the appearing of our Lord Jesus Christ, which he will display at the proper time—he who is the blessed and only Sovereign, the King of kings and Lord of lords, who alone has immortality, who dwells in unapproachable light, whom no one has ever seen or can see. To him be honor and eternal dominion. Amen.

Colossians 1:15-17   He is the image of the invisible God, the firstborn of all creation. For by him all things were created, in heaven and on earth, visible and invisible, whether thrones or dominions or rulers or authorities—all things were created through him and for him. And he is before all things, and in him all things hold together.

1 Corinthians 8:6   Yet for us there is one God, the Father, from whom are all things and for whom we exist, and one Lord, Jesus Christ, through whom are all things and through whom we exist.

Isaiah 9:6   For to us a child is born, to us a son is given; and the government shall be upon his shoulder, and his name shall be called Wonderful Counselor, Mighty God, Everlasting Father, Prince of Peace.

MAKE
JESUS YOUR LOVE

John 13:34-35 A new commandment I give to you, that you love one another: just as I have loved you, you also are to love one another. By this all people will know that you are my disciples, if you have love for one another."

1 John 4:19 We love because he first loved us.

1 John 4:16 So we have come to know and to believe the love that God has for us. God is love, and whoever abides in love abides in God, and God abides in him.

Zephaniah 3:17 The Lord your God is in your midst, a mighty one who will save; he will rejoice over you with gladness; he will quiet you by his love; he will exult over you with loud singing.

Romans 8:37-39 No, in all these things we are more than conquerors through him who loved us. For I am sure that neither death nor life, nor angels nor rulers, nor things present nor things to come, nor powers, nor height nor depth, nor anything else in all creation, will be able to separate us from the love of God in Christ Jesus our Lord.

Jeremiah 31:3 The Lord appeared to him from far away. I have loved you with an everlasting love; therefore, I have continued my faithfulness to you.

Ephesians 5:2 And walk in love, as Christ loved us and gave himself up for us, a fragrant offering and sacrifice to God.

Ephesians 3:17-19 So that Christ may dwell in your hearts through faith—that you, being rooted and grounded in love, may have strength to comprehend with all the saints what is the breadth and length and height and depth, and to know the love of Christ that surpasses knowledge, that you may be filled with all the fullness of God.

John 15:12-13 "This is my commandment, that you love one another as I have loved you. Greater love has no one than this, that someone lay down his life for his friends.

John 15:9-17 As the Father has loved me, so have I loved you. Abide in my love. If you keep my commandments, you will abide in my love, just as I have kept my Father's commandments and abide in his love. These things I have spoken to you, that my joy may be in you, and that your joy may be full. "This is my commandment, that you love one another as I have loved you. Greater love has no one than this, that someone lay down his life for his friends. ...

1 John 4:9 In this the love of God was made manifest among us, that God sent his only Son into the world, so that we might live through him.

Ephesians 2:4-5 But God, being rich in mercy, because of the great love with which he loved us, even when we were dead in our trespasses, made us alive together with Christ—by grace you have been saved—

Romans 5:5 And hope does not put us to shame, because God's love has been poured into our hearts through the Holy Spirit who has been given to us.

JESUS BRINGS PEACE

John 16:33 I have said these things to you, that in me you may have peace. In the world you will have tribulation. But take heart; I have overcome the world."

John 14:27 Peace I leave with you; my peace I give to you. Not as the world gives do I give to you. Let not your hearts be troubled, neither let them be afraid.

Romans 15:13 May the God of hope fill you with all joy and peace in believing, so that by the power of the Holy Spirit you may abound in hope.

Colossians 3:15 And let the peace of Christ rule in your hearts, to which indeed you were called in one body. And be thankful.

2 Thessalonians 3:16 Now may the Lord of peace himself give you peace at all times in every way. The Lord be with you all.

Isaiah 26:3 You keep him in perfect peace whose mind is stayed on you, because he trusts in you.

Philippians 4:6-7 Do not be anxious about anything, but in everything by prayer and supplication with thanksgiving let your requests be made known to God. And the peace of God, which surpasses all understanding, will guard your hearts and your minds in Christ Jesus.

Isaiah 53:5 But he was wounded for our transgressions; he was crushed for our iniquities; upon him was the chastisement that brought us peace, and with his stripes we are healed.

Psalm 4:8 In peace I will both lie down and sleep; for you alone, O Lord, make me dwell in safety.

2 Corinthians 13:11 Finally, brothers, rejoice. Aim for restoration, comfort one another, agree with one another, live in peace; and the God of love and peace will be with you.

1 Corinthians 1:3 Grace to you and peace from God our Father and the Lord Jesus Christ. As for the word that he sent to Israel, preaching good news of peace through Jesus Christ (he is Lord of all),

Ephesians 2:14-17 For he himself is our peace, who has made us both one and has broken down in his flesh the dividing wall of hostility by abolishing the law of commandments expressed in ordinances, that he might create in himself one new man in place of the two, so making peace, and might reconcile us both to God in one body through the cross, thereby killing the hostility. And he came and preached peace to you who were far off and peace to those who were near.

JESUS IS OUR FORGIVENESS

1 John 1:9 If we confess our sins, he is faithful and just to forgive us our sins and to cleanse us from all unrighteousness.

1 John 2:1 My little children, I am writing these things to you so that you may not sin. But if anyone does sin, we have an advocate with the Father, Jesus Christ the righteous.

Isaiah 43:25-26 "I, I am he who blots out your transgressions for my own sake, and I will not remember your sins. Put me in remembrance; let us argue together; set forth your case, that you may be proved right.

Ephesians 1:7 In him we have redemption through his blood, the forgiveness of our trespasses, according to the riches of his grace,

Isaiah 1:18 "Come now, let us reason together, says the Lord: though your sins are like scarlet, they shall be as white as snow; though they are red like crimson, they shall become like wool.

Psalm 103:12 As far as the east is from the west, so far does he remove our transgressions from us.

Romans 8:1 There is therefore now no condemnation for those who are in Christ Jesus.

Daniel 9:9 To the Lord our God belong mercy and forgiveness, for we have rebelled against Him

Hebrews 10:17 Then he adds: "I will remember their sins and their lawless deeds no more.

Acts 2:38 And Peter said to them, "Repent and be baptized every one of you in the name of Jesus Christ for the forgiveness of your sins, and you will receive the gift of the Holy Spirit.

Luke 23:34 And Jesus said, "Father, forgive them, for they know not what they do." And they cast lots to divide his garments.

Matthew 26:28 For this is my blood of the covenant, which is poured out for many for the forgiveness of sins.

Colossians 2:12 And you, who were dead in your trespasses and the uncircumcision of your flesh, God made alive together with him, having forgiven us all our trespasses,

Isaiah 55:7 Let the wicked forsake his way, and the unrighteous man his thoughts; let him return to the Lord, that he may have compassion on him, and to our God, for he will abundantly pardon.

Colossians 1:13-14 He has delivered us from the domain of darkness and transferred us to the kingdom of his beloved Son, in whom we have redemption, the forgiveness of sins.

RIGHTEOUSNESS THROUGH JESUS

Philippians 3:9 And be found in him, not having a righteousness of my own that comes from the law, but that which comes through faith in Christ, the righteousness from God that depends on faith.

2 Corinthians 5:21 For our sake he made him to be sin who knew no sin, so that in him we might become the righteousness of God.

Romans 4:3 For what does the Scripture say? "Abraham believed God, and it was counted to him as righteousness."

1 Corinthians 1:30 And because of him you are in Christ Jesus, who became to us wisdom from God, righteousness and sanctification and redemption.

Romans 10:4 For Christ is the end of the law for righteousness to everyone who believes.

Romans 3:22 The righteousness of God through faith in Jesus Christ for all who believe. For there is no distinction:

2 Corinthians 5:17 Therefore, if anyone is in Christ, he is a new creation. The old has passed away; behold, the new has come.

Romans 4:5 And to the one who does not work but believes in him who justifies the ungodly, his faith is counted as righteousness,

2 Peter 1:1 Simeon Peter, a servant and apostle of Jesus Christ, to those who have obtained a faith of equal standing with ours by the righteousness of our God and Savior Jesus Christ:

Philippians 1:11 Filled with the fruit of righteousness that comes through Jesus Christ, to the glory and praise of God.

Romans 5:17-19 [17] For if, through one man, death ruled because of that man's offense, how much more will those who receive such overflowing grace and the gift of righteousness rule in life because of one man, Jesus the Messiah! [18] Consequently, just as one offense resulted in condemnation for everyone, so one act of righteousness results in justification and life for everyone. [19] For just as through one man's disobedience many people were made sinners, so also through one man's obedience many people will be made righteous.

JESUS CAN DELIVER

Colossians 1:13 He has delivered us from the domain of darkness and transferred us to the kingdom of his beloved Son.

Galatians 5:1 For freedom Christ has set us free; stand firm therefore, and do not submit again to a yoke of slavery.

Romans 6:22 But now that you have been set free from sin and have become slaves of God, the fruit you get leads to sanctification and its end, eternal life.

Luke 4:18 "The Spirit of the Lord is upon me, because he has anointed me to proclaim good news to the poor. He has sent me to proclaim liberty to the captives and recovering of sight to the blind, to set at liberty those who are oppressed,

Isaiah 61:1 The Spirit of the Lord God is upon me, because the Lord has anointed me to bring good news to the poor; he has sent me to bind up the brokenhearted, to proclaim liberty to the captives, and the opening of the prison to those who are bound.

Psalm 144:2 He is my steadfast love and my fortress, my stronghold and my deliverer, my shield and he in whom I take refuge, who subdues peoples under me.

Psalm 18:2 The Lord is my rock and my fortress and my deliverer, my God, my rock, in whom I take refuge, my shield, and the horn of my salvation, my stronghold.

2 Samuel 22:2 As for me, I am poor and needy, but the Lord takes thought for me. You are my help and my deliverer; do not delay, O my God! he said, "The Lord is my rock and my fortress and my deliverer.

Psalm 40:17 As for me, I am poor and needy, but the Lord takes thought for me. You are my help and my deliverer; do not delay, O my God!

Psalm 18:3 The Lord is my rock and my fortress and my deliverer, my God, my rock, in whom I take refuge, my shield, and the horn of my salvation, my stronghold. I call upon the Lord, who is worthy to be praised, and I am saved from my enemies.

Galatians 5:1 For freedom Christ has set us free; stand firm therefore, and do not submit again to a yoke of slavery.

John 8:31-32 So Jesus said to the Jews who had believed in him, "If you abide in my word, you are truly my disciples, and you will know the truth, and the truth will set you free."

JESUS IS OUR EXAMPLE: FOLLOW HIM!

Ephesians 5:1-2 Therefore be imitators of God, as beloved children. And walk in love, as Christ loved us and gave himself up for us, a fragrant offering and sacrifice to God.

1 John 2:6 Whoever says he abides in him ought to walk in the same way in which he walked

Ephesians 2:10 For we are his workmanship, created in Christ Jesus for good works, which God prepared beforehand, that we should walk in them.

High 13:15 For I have given you an example, that you also should do just as I have done to you.

John 13:35 By this all people will know that you are my disciples, if you have love for one another."

1 John 3:16 By this we know love, that he laid down his life for us, and we ought to lay down our lives for the brothers.

Philippians 2:5-8 Have this mind among yourselves, which is yours in Christ Jesus, who, though he was in the form of God, did not count equality with God a thing to be grasped, but made himself nothing, taking the form of a servant, being born in the likeness of men. And being found in human form, he humbled himself by becoming obedient to the point of death, even death on a cross.

Ephesians 5:1-2 Therefore be imitators of God, as beloved children. And walk in love, as Christ loved us and gave himself up for us, a fragrant offering and sacrifice to God.

John 8:12 Again Jesus spoke to them, saying, "I am the light of the world. Whoever follows me will not walk in darkness but will have the light of life."

JESUS IS OUR FRIEND

John 15:12-16 [12] "This is my commandment: that you love one another as I have loved you. [13] No one shows[a] greater love than when he lays down his life for his friends. [14] You are my friends, if you do what I command you. [15] I don't call you servants anymore, because a servant doesn't know what his master is doing. But I've called you friends, because I've made known to you everything that I've heard from my Father.

[16] "You have not chosen me, but I have chosen you. I have appointed you to go and produce fruit that will last, so that whatever you ask the Father in my name, he will give it to you.

Hebrews 13:5 [5] Keep your lives free from the love of money, and be content with what you have, for God[a] has said, "I will never leave you or abandon you."

Revelation 3:20 [20] Look! I am standing at the door and knocking. If anyone listens to my voice and opens the door, I will come in to him and eat with him, and he will eat[a] with me.

Isaiah 54:10 For the mountains may collapse and the hills may reel, but my gracious love will not depart from you, neither will my covenant of peace totter," says the Lord, who has compassion on you.

Psalm 27:10 Though my father and my mother abandoned me, the Lord gathers me up.

John 14:18-20 [18] I'm not going to forsake you like orphans. I will come back to you.

[19] "In a little while the world will no longer see me, but you will see me. Because I live, you will live also. [20] At that time, you'll know that I am in my Father, that you are in me, and that I am in you.

Joshua 1:5 [5] No one will be victorious[a] against you for the rest of your life. I'll be with you just like I was with Moses—I'll neither fail you nor abandon you.

Psalm 145:18 The Lord remains near to all who call out to him, to everyone who calls out to him sincerely.

JESUS IS OUR BROTHER

Hebrews 2:16-18 [16] For it is clear that he did not come to help angels. No, he came to help Abraham's descendants, [17] thereby becoming like his brothers in every way, so that he could be a merciful and faithful high priest in service to God and could atone for the people's sins. [18] Because he himself suffered when he was tempted, he is able to help those who are being tempted.

Matthew 12:47-50 [47] Someone told him, "Look! Your mother and your brothers are standing outside, asking to speak to you." [48] He asked the man who told him, "Who is my mother, and who are my brothers?" [49] Then pointing with his hand at his disciples, he said, "Here are my mother and my brothers, [50] because whoever does the will of my Father in heaven is my brother and sister and mother."

JESUS AND OUR INHERITANCE

Ephesians 1:11-14 [11] In the Messiah[a] we were also chosen when we were predestined according to the purpose of the one who does everything that he wills to do, [12] so that we who had already fixed our hope on the Messiah[b] might live for his praise and glory. [13] You, too, have heard the word of truth, the gospel of your salvation. When you believed in the Messiah,[c] you were sealed with the promised Holy Spirit, [14] who is the guarantee of our inheritance until God redeems his own possession[d] for his praise and glory.

Acts 20:32 [32] "I'm now entrusting you to God and to the message of his grace, which is able to build you up and secure for you an inheritance among all who are sanctified.

1 Peter 1:3-4 [3] Blessed be the God and Father of our Lord Jesus Christ! According to his great mercy, he has caused us to be born again to a living hope through the resurrection of Jesus Christ from the dead, [4] to an inheritance that is imperishable, undefiled, and unfading, kept in heaven for you,

Revelation 21:7 The one who conquers will have this heritage, and I will be his God and he will be my son.

Colossians 3:24 Knowing that from the Lord you will receive the inheritance as your reward. You are serving the Lord Christ.

Galatians 3:29 And if you are Christ's, then you are Abraham's offspring, heirs according to promise.

John 14:1-4 [14] "Don't let your hearts be troubled. Believe[a] in God, believe also in me. [2] There are many rooms in my Father's house. If there weren't, I wouldn't have told you that I am going away to prepare a place for you, would I? [3] And since[b] I'm going away to prepare a place for you, I'll come back again and welcome you into my presence, so that you may be where I am. [4] You know where I am going, and you know the way."

WE CAN BE SECURE IN JESUS

John 3:16 "For God so loved the world, that he gave his only Son, that whoever believes in him should not perish but have eternal life.

Philippians 4:19 And my God will supply every need of yours according to his riches in glory in Christ Jesus.

Romans 8:38-39 For I am sure that neither death nor life, nor angels nor rulers, nor things present nor things to come, nor powers, nor height nor depth, nor anything else in all creation, will be able to separate us from the love of God in Christ Jesus our Lord.

Romans 6:23 For the wages of sin is death, but the free gift of God is eternal life in Christ Jesus our Lord.

Hebrews 7:25 Consequently, he is able to save to the uttermost those who draw near to God through him, since he always lives to make intercession for them.

John 6:37 All that the Father gives me will come to me, and whoever comes to me I will never cast out.

2 Thessalonians 3:3 But the Lord is faithful. He will establish you and guard you against the evil one.

Philippians 4:6 Do not be anxious about anything, but in everything by prayer and supplication with thanksgiving let your requests be made known to God.

2 Corinthians 1:22 And who has also put his seal on us and given us his Spirit in our hearts as a guarantee.

John 10:28-29 I give them eternal life, and they will never perish, and no one will snatch them out of my hand. My Father, who has given them to me, is greater than all, and no one is able to snatch them out of the Father's hand.

Psalm 32:7 You are a hiding place for me; you preserve me from trouble; you surround me with shouts of deliverance.

IN JESUS WE ARE SUFFICIENT

2 Corinthians 12:9 But he said to me, "My grace is sufficient for you, for my power is made perfect in weakness." Therefore, I will boast all the more gladly of my weaknesses, so that the power of Christ may rest upon me.

2 Corinthians 3:5 Not that we are sufficient in ourselves to claim anything as coming from us, but our sufficiency is from God,

John 15:5 I am the vine; you are the branches. Whoever abides in me and I in him, he it is that bears much fruit, for apart from me you can do nothing.

Philippians 4:13 I am the vine; you are the branches. Whoever abides in me and I in him, he it is that bears much fruit, for apart from me you can do nothing.

2 Corinthians 9:8 And God is able to make all grace abound to you, so that having all sufficiency in all things at all times, you may abound in every good work.

Philippians 4:19 And my God will supply every need of yours according to his riches in glory in Christ Jesus.

2 Corinthians 12:9-10 But he said to me, "My grace is sufficient for you, for my power is made perfect in weakness." Therefore, I will boast all the more gladly of my weaknesses, so that the power of Christ may rest upon me. For the sake of Christ, then, I am content with weaknesses, insults, hardships, persecutions, and calamities. For when I am weak, then I am strong.

ARE YOU DEPRESSED?

John 14:1-4 "Don't let your hearts be troubled. Believe[a] in God, believe also in me. [2] There are many rooms in my Father's house. If there weren't, I wouldn't have told you that I am going away to prepare a place for you, would I? [3] And since[b] I'm going away to prepare a place for you, I'll come back again and welcome you into my presence, so that you may be where I am. [4] You know where I am going, and you know the way."

John 14:27 [27] I'm leaving you at peace. I'm giving you my own peace. I'm not giving it to you as the world gives. So don't let your hearts be troubled, and don't be afraid.

2 Corinthians 4:8-12, 16-18 [8] In every way we're troubled but not crushed, frustrated but not in despair, [9] persecuted but not abandoned, struck down but not destroyed. [10] We are always carrying around the death of Jesus in our bodies, so that the life of Jesus may be clearly shown in our bodies. [11] While we are alive, we are constantly being handed over to death for Jesus' sake, so that the life of Jesus may be clearly shown in our mortal bodies. [12] And so death is at work in us, but life is at work[a] in you.

[16] That's why we are not discouraged. No, even if outwardly we are wearing out, inwardly we are being renewed each and every day. [17] This light, temporary nature of our suffering is producing for us an everlasting weight of glory, far beyond any comparison, [18] because we do not look for things that can be seen but for things that cannot be seen. For things that can be seen are temporary, but things that cannot be seen are eternal.

1 Peter 1:6-9 [6] You greatly rejoice in this, even though you have to suffer various kinds of trials for a little while, [7] so that your genuine faith, which is more valuable than gold that perishes when tested by fire, may result in praise, glory, and honor when Jesus, the Messiah,[a] is revealed. [8] Though you have not seen[b] him, you love him. And even though you do not see him now, you believe in him and rejoice with an indescribable and glorious joy, [9] because you are receiving the goal of your faith, the salvation of your souls.

Philippians 4:6-9 [6] Never worry about anything. Instead, in every situation let your petitions be made known to God through prayers and requests, with thanksgiving. [7] Then God's peace, which goes far beyond anything we can imagine, will guard your hearts and minds in union with the Messiah[a] Jesus. [8] Finally, brothers, whatever is true, whatever is honorable, whatever is fair, whatever is pure, whatever is acceptable, whatever is commendable, if there is anything of excellence and if there is anything praiseworthy—keep thinking about these things. [9] Likewise, keep practicing these things: what you have learned, received, heard, and seen in me. Then the God of peace will be with you.

ARE YOU FEELING LONELY?

Deuteronomy 31:6 [6] Be strong and courageous. Don't fear or tremble before them, because the Lord your God will be the one who keeps on walking with you—he won't leave you or abandon you."

Psalm 27:10 Though my father and mother forsake me, the LORD will receive me.

Psalm 25:16 Turn to me and be gracious to me, for I am lonely and afflicted.

Matthew 28:20 Turn to me and be gracious to me, for I am lonely and afflicted.

Isaiah 41:10 So do not fear, for I am with you; do not be dismayed, for I am your God. I will strengthen you and help you; I will uphold you with my righteous right hand.

1 Peter 5:7 Cast all your anxiety on him because he cares for you.

Psalm 68:5-6 A father to the fatherless, a defender of widows, is God in his holy dwelling. **6** God sets the lonely in families; he leads out the prisoners with singing; but the rebellious live in a sun-scorched land.

Proverbs 18:24 One who has unreliable friends soon comes to ruin, but there is a friend who sticks closer than a brother.

Psalm 147:3 He heals the brokenhearted and binds up their wounds.

Isaiah 49:15 "Can a woman forget her nursing child, or have no compassion for the child of her womb? Even these mothers may forget; But as for me, I'll never forget you!

ARE YOU
FEELING DISSATISFIED?

Psalm 34:10 Young lions lack and go hungry, but those who seek the Lord will never lack any good thing.

Philippians 4:11-13 [11] I am not saying this because I am in any need, for I have learned to be content in whatever situation I am in. [12] I know how to be humble, and I know how to prosper. In each and every situation I have learned the secret of being full and of going hungry, of having too much and of having too little. [13] I can do all things through him[a] who strengthens me.

Hebrews 13:5 [5] Keep your lives free from the love of money, and be content with what you have, for God[a] has said, "I will never leave you or abandon you."[b]

Ecclesiastes 5:10 Whoever loves money will never have enough money. Whoever loves luxury will not be content with abundance. This also is pointless.

1 Timothy 6:6-7 Of course, godliness with contentment does bring a great profit. [7] Nothing to this world we bring; from it take we nothing.

Psalm 107:9 He has satisfied the one who thirsts, filling the hungry with what is good.

Psalm 63:1-5 God, you are my God! I will fervently seek you. My soul thirsts for you; my flesh longs for you in a dry, weary, and parched land. [2] So I have looked for you in the sanctuary, to behold your power and glory. [3] Because your gracious love is better than life itself, my lips will praise you. [4] So I will bless you as long as I live; I will lift up my hands in your name. [5] Just as I am satisfied with the choicest of foods,[a] so my lips will praise you joyfully.

ARE YOU FEELING JUDGED?

1 John 1:9 [9] If we make it our habit to confess our sins, in his faithful righteousness he forgives us for those sins and cleanses us from all unrighteousness.

Micah 7:19 He will again show us compassion; he will subdue our iniquities. You will hurl all their sins into the deepest sea.

Romans 8:1-2 Therefore, there is now no condemnation for those who are in union with the Messiah[a] Jesus.[b] [2] For the Spirit's law of life in the Messiah[c] Jesus has set me[d] free from the Law of sin and death.

Isaiah 50:7 For the Lord God helps me, so I won't be disgraced. Therefore, I've made my face like flint, and I know that I won't be put to shame."

Psalm 103:10-12 He neither deals with us according to our sins, nor repays us equivalent to our iniquity.[11] As high as heaven rises above earth, so his gracious love strengthens[a] those who fear him. [12] As distant as the east is from the west, that is how far he has removed our sins from us.

John 3:16-18 [16] "For this is how God loved the world: He gave his uniquely existing Son so that everyone who believes in him would not be lost but have eternal life. [17] Because God sent the Son into the world, not to condemn the world, but that the world would be saved through him. [18] Whoever believes in him is not condemned, but whoever does not believe has already been condemned, because he has not believed in the name of God's uniquely existing Son.

John 5:24 [24] "Truly, I tell all of you[a] emphatically, whoever hears what I say and believes in the one who sent me has eternal life and will not be judged, but has passed from death to life.

Hebrews 8:12 For I will be merciful regarding their wrong deeds, and

I will never again remember their sins."

Isaiah 43:25 "I, I am the one who blots out your transgression for my own sake, and I'll remember your sins no more.

Isaiah 55:6-9 "Seek the Lord while he[a] may be found, call upon him while he is near. [7] Let the wicked forsake his way, and the unrighteous person his thoughts. Let him return to the Lord, So he'll have mercy upon him, and to our God, for he'll pardon abundantly. [8] For my thoughts are not your thoughts, nor are your ways my ways," declares the Lord. [9] "For just as[b] the heavens are higher than the earth, so are my ways higher than your ways,

and my thoughts than your thoughts.

DO YOU FEEL BEWILDERED AND CONFUSED?

Provers 3:5-6 Trust in the Lord with all your heart, and do not lean on your own understanding. In all your ways acknowledge him, and he will make straight your paths.

Philippians 4:8-9 Finally, brothers, whatever is true, whatever is honorable, whatever is just, whatever is pure, whatever is lovely, whatever is commendable, if there is any excellence, if there is anything worthy of praise, think about these things. What you have learned and received and heard and seen in me—practice these things, and the God of peace will be with you.

Psalm 32:8 I will instruct you and teach you concerning the path you should walk; I will direct you with my eye.

Isaiah 30:21 [21] And whether you turn to the right or turn to the left, your ears will hear a message behind you: "This is the way, walk in it."

Psalm 119:34 Give me understanding, that I may keep your law and observe it with my whole heart.

Proverbs 28:5 Evil men do not understand justice, but those who seek the Lord understand it completely.

OVERCOME BY TEMPTATION?

1 Corinthians 10:13 No temptation has overtaken you that is not common to man. God is faithful, and he will not let you be tempted beyond your ability, but with the temptation he will also provide the way of escape, that you may be able to endure it.

Hebrews 4:15 For we do not have a high priest who is unable to sympathize with our weaknesses, but one who in every respect has been tempted as we are, yet without sin.

Matthew 26:41 Watch and pray that you may not enter into temptation. The spirit indeed is willing, but the flesh is weak."

1 Timothy 6:9 But those who desire to be rich fall into temptation, into a snare, into many senseless and harmful desires that plunge people into ruin and destruction.

1 Peter 5:8 Be sober-minded; be watchful. Your adversary the devil prowls around like a roaring lion, seeking someone to devour.

1 Corinthians 6:18-20 Flee from sexual immorality. Every other sin a person commits is outside the body, but the sexually immoral person sins against his own body. Or do you not know that your body is a temple of the Holy Spirit within you, whom you have from God? You are not your own, for you were bought with a price. So, glorify God in your body.

Luke 22:46 And he said to them, "Why are you sleeping? Rise and pray that you may not enter into temptation."

Luke 4:13 And when the devil had ended every temptation, he departed from him until an opportune time.

Mark 14:38 Watch and pray that you may not enter into temptation. The spirit indeed is willing, but the flesh is weak."

1 John 2:15-17 Do not love the world or the things in the world. If anyone loves the world, the love of the Father is not in him. For all that is in the world—the desires of the flesh and the desires of the eyes and pride in possessions—is not from the Father but is from the world. And the world is passing away along with its desires, but whoever does the will of God abides forever.

James 1:13-16 Let no one say when he is tempted, "I am being tempted by God," for God cannot be tempted with evil, and he himself tempts no one. But each person is tempted when he is lured and enticed by his own desire. Then desire when it has conceived gives birth to sin, and sin when it is fully grown brings forth death. Do not be deceived, my beloved brothers.

Galatians 6:1 Brothers,[a] if anyone is caught in any transgression, you who are spiritual should restore him in a spirit of gentleness. Keep watch on yourself, lest you too be tempted.

HOW TO MANAGE
OUR ANGER

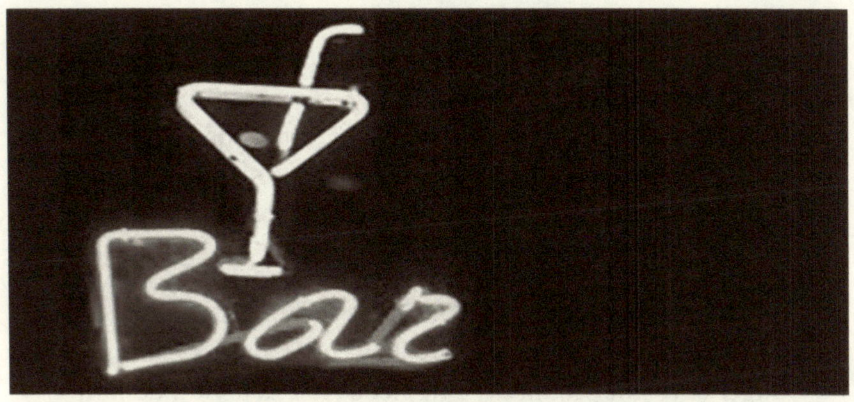

Luke 6:27-29 [27] "But I say to you who are listening: Love your enemies. Do good to those who hate you. [28] Bless those who curse you. Pray for those who insult you. [29] If someone strikes you on the cheek, offer him the other one as well, and if someone takes your coat, don't keep back your shirt, either.

Proverbs 22:25 A soft answer turns away wrath, but a harsh word stirs up anger.

Romans 12:19 Beloved, never avenge yourselves, but leave it to the wrath of God, for it is written, "Vengeance is mine, I will repay, says the Lord."

Ephesians 4:25-27 Therefore, having put away falsehood, let each one of you speak the truth with his neighbor, for we are members one of another. Be angry and do not sin; do not let the sun go down on your anger and give no opportunity to the devil.

Philippians 4:13 I can do all things through him who strengthens me.

Psalm 4:4 Be angry, and do not sin; ponder in your own hearts on your beds and be silent.

Philippians 2:3 Do nothing from rivalry or conceit, but in humility count others more significant than yourselves.

Luke 6:27 "But I say to you who hear, Love your enemies, do good to those who hate you,

Matthew 5:22-24 But I say to you that everyone who is angry with his brother will be liable to judgment; whoever insults his brother will be liable to the council; and whoever says, 'You fool!' will be liable to the hell of fire. So, if you are offering your gift at the altar and there remember that your brother has something against you, leave your gift there before the altar and go. First be reconciled to your brother, and then come and offer your gift.

[19] You must understand this, my dear brothers. Everyone should be quick to listen, slow to speak, and slow to get angry. [20] For human anger does not produce the righteousness that God desires.

Matt 6:14 [14] Because if you forgive people their offenses, your heavenly Father will also forgive you.

DO YOU FEEL REBELLIOUS?

Hebrews 12:5-6 And ye have forgotten the exhortation which speaketh unto you as unto children, My son, despise not thou the chastening of the Lord, nor faint when thou art rebuked of him: For whom the Lord loveth he chasteneth, and scourgeth every son whom he receiveth.

Psalm 119:67 Before I was afflicted I went astray, but now I obey your word.

2 Timothy 4:3-4 For the time will come when they will not tolerate sound doctrine, but according to their own desires, will multiply teachers for themselves because they have an itch to hear something new. They will turn away from hearing the truth and will turn aside to myths.

Matthew 7:21-23 Not everyone that saith unto me, Lord, Lord, shall enter into the kingdom of heaven; but he that doeth the will of my Father which is in heaven. Many will say to me in that day, Lord, Lord, have we not prophesied in thy name? and in thy name have cast out devils? and in thy name done many wonderful works? And then will I profess unto them, I never knew you: depart from me, ye that work iniquity.

Proverbs 28:9 The one who turns away his ear from hearing the law, even his prayer is an abomination.

2 Timothy 3:1-5 But understand this, that in the last days there will come times of difficulty. For people will be lovers of self, lovers of money, proud, arrogant, abusive, disobedient to their parents, ungrateful, unholy, heartless, unappeasable, slanderous, without self-control, brutal, not loving good, treacherous, reckless, swollen with conceit, lovers of pleasure rather than lovers of God, having the appearance of godliness, but denying its power. Avoid such people.

Hebrews 13:17 [17] Continue to follow and be submissive to your leaders, since they are watching over your souls as those who will have to give a word of explanation. By doing this, you will be letting them carry out their duties joyfully, and not with grief, for that would be harmful for you.

Isaiah 50:5-6 My Lord God[a] has opened my ears, and I did not rebel; I did not shrink back. [6] I gave my back to those who beat me and my cheeks to those who pulled out my beard.[b] I did not turn away[c] my face from insults and spitting.

Ephesians 4:17-24 [17] Therefore, I tell you and insist on[a] in the Lord not to live any longer like the gentiles live, thinking worthless thoughts.[b] [18] They are darkened in their understanding and separated from the life of God because of their ignorance and hardness of heart. [19] Since they have lost all sense of shame, they have abandoned themselves to sensuality and practice every kind of sexual perversion without restraint. [20] However, that is not the way you came to know the Messiah.[c] [21] Surely you have listened to him and have been taught by him, since truth is in Jesus. [22] Regarding your former way of life, you were taught[d] to strip off your old nature, which is being ruined by its deceptive desires, [23] to be renewed in your mental attitude, [24] and to clothe yourselves with the new nature, which was created according to God's image[e] in righteousness and true holiness.

WHAT TO DO
WHEN YOU FEEL AFRIAD

Isaiah 51:7-8 Listen to me, you who know righteousness, you people who have my instruction[a] in their hearts. Don't fear the insults of mortals, and don't be dismayed at their hateful words.[b]
[8] For moths will eat them up just like a garment, and worms will devour them like wool; but my deliverance will last[c] forever, and my salvation to all generations.

Matthew 8:26 [26] He asked them, "Why are you afraid, you who have little faith?" Then he got up and rebuked the winds and the sea, and there was a great calm.

2 Timothy 1:7 [7] For God did not give us a spirit of timidity but one of power, love, and self-discipline.

Romans 8:15 [15] For you have not received a spirit of slavery that leads you into fear again. Instead, you have received the Spirit of adoption by whom we cry out, "Abba![a] Father!"

1 John 4:18 [18] There is no fear where love exists.[a] Rather, perfect love banishes fear, for fear involves punishment, and the person who lives in fear has not been perfected in love.

Proverbs 3:25-26 Do not be afraid of sudden disaster, or the devastation that comes to the wicked. [26] Indeed, the Lord will be your confidence, and he will keep your foot from being caught.

Psalm 56:11 In God I will put my trust. I will not fear what mortal man can do to me.

Psalm 18:1-2 He said: "I love you, Lord, my strength.
[2] The Lord is my rock, my fortress, my deliverer, my God, my stronghold[a] in whom I take refuge, my shield, the glory of my salvation, and my high tower."

Psalm 27:1 The Lord is my light and my salvation— whom will I fear? The Lord is the strength of my life; of whom will I be afraid?

Hebrews 13:6 [6] Hence we can confidently say, "The Lord is my helper; I will not be afraid. What can anyone do to me?"

2 Corinthians 12:9-10 but he has told me, "My grace is all you need, because my power is perfected in weakness." Therefore, I will most happily boast about my weaknesses, so that the Messiah's[a] power may rest on me. [10] That is why I take such pleasure in weaknesses, insults, hardships, persecutions, and difficulties for the Messiah's[b] sake, for when I am weak, then I am strong.

Isaiah 41:10-13 Fear not, for I am with you; be not dismayed, for I am your God; I will strengthen you, I will help you, I will uphold you with my righteous right hand.

Psalm 118:6 The Lord is with me. I will not be afraid. What can people do to me?

Psalm 34:4 I sought the Lord and he answered me. He delivered me from all of my fears.

Psalm 56:3 On days when I am afraid, I put my trust in you.

Mark 5:36 [36] But when Jesus heard[a] what they said, he told the synagogue leader, "Stop being afraid! Just keep on believing."

Psalm 46:1 God is our refuge and strength; a great help in times of distress.

Deuteronomy 31:8 [8] Indeed, the Lord is the one who will keep on walking in front of you. He'll be with you and won't leave you or abandon you, so never be afraid and never be dismayed."

Isaiah 54:4 "Don't be afraid, because you won't be ashamed; don't fear shame, for you won't be humiliated—because you will forget the disgrace of your youth, and the reproach of your widowhood you will remember no more.

Are You Anxious?

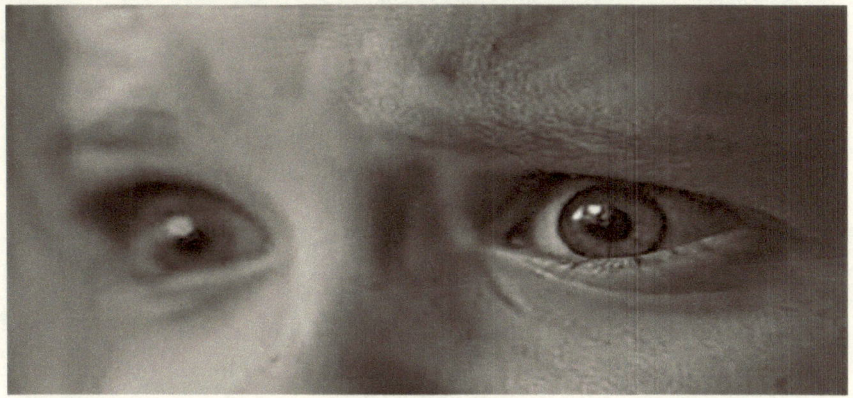

Psalm 23 The Lord *is* my shepherd; I shall not want. ² He maketh me to lie down in green pastures: he leadeth me beside the still waters. ³ He restoreth my soul: he leadeth me in the paths of righteousness for his name's sake. ⁴ Yea, though I walk through the valley of the shadow of death, I will fear no evil: for thou *art* with me; thy rod and thy staff they comfort me. ⁵ Thou preparest a table before me in the presence of mine enemies: thou anointest my head with oil; my cup runneth over. ⁶ Surely goodness and mercy shall follow me all the days of my life: and I will dwell in the house of the Lord forever.

1 Peter 5:7 Cast all your anxieties on him, because he cares for you.

Philippians 4:6-7 Do not be anxious about anything, but in everything by prayer and supplication with thanksgiving let your requests be made known to God. And the peace of God, which surpasses all understanding, will guard your hearts and your minds in Christ Jesus.

Matthew 11:28-30 Come to me, all who labor and are heavy laden, and I will give you rest. Take my yoke upon you, and learn from me, for I am gentle and lowly in heart, and you will find rest for your souls. For my yoke is easy, and my burden is light."

Jeremiah 29:11 For I know the plans I have for you, declares the Lord, plans for welfare and not for evil, to give you a future and a hope.

Romans 8:28 And we know that for those who love God all things work together for good, for those who are called according to his purpose.

Isaiah 40:31 But they who wait for the Lord shall renew their strength; they shall mount up with wings like eagles; they shall run and not be weary; they shall walk and not faint.

Isaiah 26:3 You keep him in perfect peace whose mind is stayed on you, because he trusts in you.

Deuteronomy 31:8 It is the Lord who goes before you. He will be with you; he will not leave you or forsake you. Do not fear or be dismayed."

2 Corinthians 12:9-10 [9] but he has told me, "My grace is all you need, because my power is perfected in weakness." Therefore, I will most happily boast about my weaknesses, so that the Messiah's[a] power may rest on me. [10] That is why I take such pleasure in weaknesses, insults, hardships, persecutions, and difficulties for the Messiah's[b] sake, for when I am weak, then I am strong.

Romans 8:31-39 [31] What shall we then say to these things? If God *be* for us, who *can be* against us? [32] He that spared not his own Son, but delivered him up for us all, how shall he not with him also freely give us all things? [33] Who shall lay anything to the charge of God's elect? *It is* God that justifieth. [34] Who *is* he that condemneth? *It is* Christ that died, yea rather, that is risen again, who is even at the right hand of God, who also maketh intercession for us. [35] Who shall separate us from the love of Christ? *shall* tribulation, or distress, or persecution, or famine, or nakedness, or peril, or sword? [36] As it is written, For thy sake we are killed all the day long; we are accounted as sheep for the slaughter. [37] Nay, in all these things we are more than conquerors through him that loved us. [38] For I am persuaded, that neither death, nor life, nor angels, nor principalities, nor powers, nor things present, nor things to come, [39] nor height, nor depth, nor any other creature, shall be able to separate us from the love of God, which is in Christ Jesus our Lord.

Psalm 31:24 Be strong, and let your heart be courageous, all you who put your hope in the Lord.

Romans 5:3-5 [3] Not only that, but we also boast[a] in our sufferings, knowing that suffering produces endurance, [4] endurance produces character, and character produces hope. [5] Now this hope does not disappoint us, because God's love has been poured out into our hearts by the Holy Spirit, who has been given to us.

Romans 12:12 Rejoice in hope, be patient in tribulations, be constant in prayer.

Psalm 37:7 Be still before the Lord and wait patiently for him; fret not yourself over the one who prospers in his way, over the man who carries out evil devices!

2 Peter 3:9 The Lord is not slow to fulfill his promise as some count slowness, but is patient toward you, not wishing that any should perish, but that all should reach repentance.

1 Peter 2:19-23 For this is a gracious thing, when, mindful of God, one endures sorrows while suffering unjustly. For what credit is it if, when you sin and are beaten for it, you endure? But if when you do good and suffer for it you endure, this is a gracious thing in the sight of God. For to this you have been called, because Christ also suffered for you, leaving you an example, so that you might follow in his steps. He committed no sin, neither was deceit found in his mouth. When he was reviled, he did not revile in return; when he suffered, he did not threaten, but continued entrusting himself to him who judges justly.

2 Timothy 2:24 And the Lord's servant must not be quarrelsome but kind to everyone, able to teach, patiently enduring evil,

1 Corinthians 13:4-5 Love is patient and kind; love does not envy or boast; it is not arrogant or rude. It does not insist on its own way; it is not irritable or resentful;

Isaiah 40:28-31 Don't you know? Haven't you heard? The Lord is the eternal God, the Creator of the ends of the earth. He does not grow tired or weary; and[a] his understanding cannot be fathomed. [29] He's the[b] one who gives might to the faint, renewing strength for the powerless. [30] Even boys grow tired and weary, and young men collapse and fall, [31] but those who keep waiting for the Lord will renew their strength. Then[c] they'll soar on wings like eagles; they'll run and not grow weary; they'll walk and not grow tired."

Psalm 27:14 Wait on the Lord.   Be courageous, and he will strengthen your heart. Wait on the Lord!

Galatians 6:9 [9] Let's not get tired of doing what is good, for at the right time we will reap a harvest—if we do not give up.

Ecclesiastes 7:8-9 The conclusion of something is better than its beginning, and a patient attitude[a] is more valuable than a proud one. [9] Never be in a hurry to become internally angry, since anger settles down in the lap of fools.

Colossians 3:12-13 [12] Therefore, as God's chosen ones, holy and loved, clothe yourselves with compassion, kindness, humility, meekness,[a] and patience. [13] Be tolerant of one another and forgive each other if anyone has a complaint against another. Just as the Lord[b] has forgiven you, you also should forgive.[c]

Romans 12:12 [12] Be joyful in hope, patient in trouble, and persistent in prayer.

Psalm 37:7-9 Be silent in the Lord's presence and wait patiently for him. Don't be angry because of the one whose way prospers or the one who implements evil schemes. [8] Calm your anger and abandon wrath. Don't be angry—it only leads to evil. [9] Those who do evil will perish. But those who wait[a] on the Lord will inherit the land.

1 Thessalonians 5:14 [14] We urge you, brothers, to admonish[a] those who are idle,[b] cheer up those who are discouraged, and help those who are weak. Be patient with everyone.

James 1:2-4 [2] Consider it pure joy, my brothers, when you are involved in various trials, [3] because you know that the testing of your faith produces endurance. [4] But you must let endurance have its full effect, so that you may be mature and complete, lacking nothing.

WHAT TO DO WHEN YOU ARE LUKEWARM SPIRITUALLY

2 Timothy 4:3 For the time is coming when people will not endure sound teaching, but having itching ears they will accumulate for themselves teachers to suit their own passions,

Hebrews 5:11-12 About this we have much to say, and it is hard to explain, since you have become dull of hearing. For though by this time, you ought to be teachers, you need someone to teach you again the basic principles of the oracles of God. You need milk, not solid food,

1 John 2:15-17 [15] Stop loving[a] the world and the things that are in the world. If anyone persists in loving the world, the Father's love is not in him. [16] For everything that is in the world—the desire for fleshly gratification,[b] the desire for possessions,[c] and worldly arrogance—is not from the Father but is from the world. [17] And the world and its desires are fading away, but the person who does God's will remains forever.

Acts 2:38 And Peter said to them, "Repent and be baptized every one of you in the name of Jesus Christ for the forgiveness of your sins, and you will receive the gift of the Holy Spirit.

Titus 1:16 They profess to know God, but they deny him by their works. They are detestable, disobedient, unfit for any good work.

Hebrews 3:12-13 [12] See to it, my brothers, that no evil, unbelieving heart is found in any of you, as shown by your turning away from the living God. [13] Instead, continue to encourage one another every day, as long as it is called "Today," so that none of you may be hardened by the deceitfulness of sin.

Acts 3:19 Repent therefore, and turn again, that your sins may be blotted out,

Revelations 2:5 Remember therefore from where you have fallen; repent and do the works you did at first. If not, I will come to you and remove your lampstand from its place, unless you repent.

Ezekiel 18:30-32 "Therefore I will judge you, O house of Israel, everyone according to his ways, declares the Lord God. Repent and turn from all your transgressions, lest iniquity be your ruin. Cast away from you all the transgressions that you have committed and make yourselves a new heart and a new spirit! Why will you die, O house of Israel? For I have no pleasure in the death of anyone, declares the Lord God; so turn, and live."

BIBLE VERSES
FOR THOSE IN GRIEF

Revelation 21:4 He will wipe away every tear from their eyes, and death shall be no more, neither shall there be mourning, nor crying, nor pain anymore, for the former things have passed away."

Psalm 147:3 He heals the brokenhearted and binds up their wounds.

Psalm 77:2-3 In the day of my trouble I seek the Lord; in the night my hand is stretched out without wearying; my soul refuses to be comforted. When I remember God, I moan; when I meditate, my spirit faints.

John 16:33 I have said these things to you, that in me you may have peace. In the world you will have tribulation. But take heart; I have overcome the world."

1 Thessalonians 4:13-18 But we do not want you to be uninformed, brothers, about those who are asleep, that you may not grieve as others do who have no hope. For since we believe that Jesus died and rose again, even so, through Jesus, God will bring with him those who have fallen asleep. For this we declare to you by a word from the Lord, that we who are alive, who are left until the coming of the Lord, will not precede those who have fallen asleep. For the Lord himself will descend from heaven with a cry of command, with the voice of an archangel, and with the sound of the trumpet of God. And the dead in Christ will rise first. Then we who are alive, who are left, will be caught up together with them in the clouds to meet the Lord in the air, and so we will always be with the Lord. ...

John 3:16 "For God so loved the world, that he gave his only Son, that whoever believes in him should not perish but have eternal life.

2 Corinthians 1:3-7 [3] Blessed be the God and Father of our Lord Jesus Christ, the Father of mercies and God of all comfort, [4] who comforts us in all our affliction, so that we may be able to comfort those who are in any affliction, with the comfort with which we ourselves are comforted by God. [5] For as we share abundantly in Christ's sufferings, so through Christ we share abundantly in comfort too.[a] 6 If we are afflicted, it is for your comfort and salvation; and if we are comforted, it is for your comfort, which you experience when you patiently endure the same sufferings that we suffer. 7 Our hope for you is unshaken, for we know that as you share in our sufferings, you will also share in our comfort.

John 11:25 Jesus said to her, "I am the resurrection and the life. Whoever believes in me, though he die, yet shall he live,

Isaiah 25:8 he has swallowed up[a] death forever! Then the Lord God will wipe away the tears from all faces, and he will take away the disgrace of his people from the entire earth." for the Lord has spoken.

Isaiah 61:1-3 "The Spirit of the Lord[a] is upon me, because the Lord has anointed me; he has sent me to bring good news to the oppressed and[b] to bind up the brokenhearted, to proclaim freedom for the captives, and release from darkness[c] for the prisoners; 2 to proclaim the year of the Lord's favor, the[d] day of vengeance of our God; to comfort all who mourn; 3 to provide for those who grieve in Zion—to bestow on them a crown of beauty instead of ashes, the oil of gladness instead of mourning, a mantle of praise instead of a spirit of despair."

Ecclesiastes 3:1-17 For everything there is a season, and a time for every matter under heaven:

2 a time to be born, and a time to die; a time to plant, and a time to pluck up what is planted; 3 a time to kill, and a time to heal; a time to break down, and a time to build up; 4 a time to weep, and a time to laugh; a time to mourn, and a time to dance; 5 a time to cast away stones, and a time to gather stones together; a time to embrace, and a time to refrain from embracing; 6 a time to seek, and a time to lose; a time to keep, and a time to cast away; 7 a time to tear, and a time to sew; a time to keep silence, and a time to speak; 8 a time to love, and a time to hate; a time for war, and a time for peace.

Isaiah 43:2 When you pass through the waters, I'll be with you; and through the rivers, they won't sweep over you; when you walk

through fire you won't be scorched, and the flame won't set you
ablaze.

Isaiah 25:8 He has swallowed up[a] death forever!
Then the Lord God will wipe away the tears from all faces, and he
will take away the disgrace of his people from the entire earth." for
the Lord has spoken.

Isaiah 61:1-3 "The Spirit of the Lord[a] is upon me, because
the Lord has anointed me; he has sent me to bring good news to the
oppressed and[b] to bind up the brokenhearted, to proclaim freedom
for the captives, and release from darkness[c] for the prisoners;
[2] to proclaim the year of the Lord's favor, the[d] day of vengeance of
our God; to comfort all who mourn; [3] to provide for those who grieve
in Zion—to bestow on them a crown of beauty instead of ashes, the
oil of gladness instead of mourning, a mantle of praise instead of a
spirit of despair."

Psalm 23 The Lord is the one who is shepherding me; I lack nothing.
[2] He causes me to lie down in pastures of green grass; he guides me
beside quiet waters. [3] He revives my life; he leads me in pathways that
are righteous for the sake of his name.[a] [4] Even when I walk through
a valley of deep darkness,[b] I will not be afraid because you are with
me. Your rod and your staff—they comfort me. [5] You prepare a table
before me, even in the presence of my enemies. You anoint my head
with oil; my cup overflows.
[6] Truly, goodness and gracious love will pursue me all the days of my
life, and I will remain in[c] the Lord's Temple forever.[d]

Matthew 5:4 "How blessed are those who mourn, because it is they
who will be comforted!

John 14:1-4 [14] "Don't let your hearts be troubled. Believe[a] in God,
believe also in me. [2] There are many rooms in my Father's house.
If there weren't, I wouldn't have told you that I am going away to
prepare a place for you, would I? [3] And since[b] I'm going away to
prepare a place for you, I'll come back again and welcome you into
my presence, so that you may be where I am. [4] You know where I am
going, and you know the way."

John 11:25-26 [superscript]25[/superscript] Jesus told her, "I am the resurrection and the life.[a] The person who believes in me, even though he dies, will live. [superscript]26[/superscript] Indeed, everyone who lives and believes in me will never die.

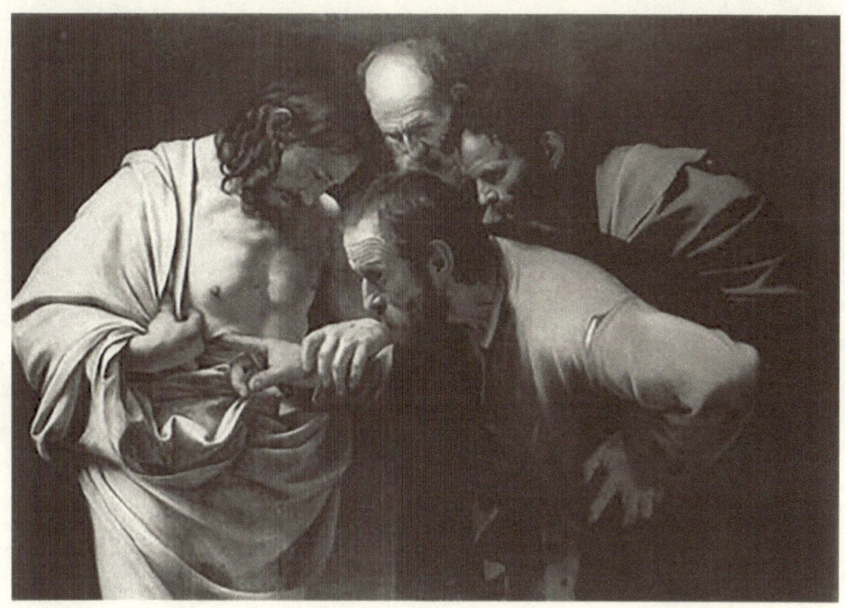

Do you believe that?"

1 Corinthians 15:51-57 [superscript]51[/superscript] Let me tell you a secret. Not all of us will die,[a] but all of us will be changed— [superscript]52[/superscript] in a moment, faster than an eye can blink, at the sound of the last trumpet. Indeed, that trumpet[b] will sound, and then the dead will be raised never to decay, and we will be changed. [superscript]53[/superscript] For what is decaying must be clothed with what cannot decay, and what is dying must be clothed with what cannot die. [superscript]54[/superscript] Now, when what is decaying is clothed with what cannot decay, and what is dying is clothed with what cannot die, then the written word will be fulfilled: "Death has been swallowed up by victory!"[c]

[superscript]55[/superscript] "Where, O death, is your victory? Where, O death, is your sting?"[d] [superscript]56[/superscript] Now death's stinger is sin, and sin's power is the Law. [superscript]57[/superscript] But thanks be to God, who gives us the victory through our Lord Jesus the Messiah![e]

WHAT TO DO WHEN YOU ARE IN DOUBT ABOUT GOD

Proverbs 3:5-8 Trust in the Lord with all your heart, and do not depend on your own understanding. [6] In all your ways acknowledge him, and he will make your paths straight. [7] Do not be wise in your own opinion. Fear the Lord and turn away from evil. [8] This will bring healing to your body, and refreshment to your bones.

Romans 10:17 [17] Consequently, faith results from listening, and listening results through the word of the Messiah.

Matthew 14:28-31 [28] Peter answered him, "Lord, if it's you, order me to come to you on the water."[29] Jesus[a] said, "Come on!" So Peter got down out of the boat, started walking on the water, and came[b] to Jesus. [30] But when he noticed the strong[c] wind, he was frightened. As he began to sink, he shouted, "Lord, save me!" [31] At once Jesus reached out his hand, caught him, and asked him, "You who have so little faith, why did you doubt?"

Mark 9:21-24 [21] Then Jesus[a] asked his father, "How long has this been happening to him?" He said, "Since he was a child. [22] The spirit[b] has often thrown him into fire and into water to destroy him. But if you are able to do anything, have pity on us and help us!" [23] Jesus told him, "'If you are able?' Everything is possible for the person who believes!" [24] With tears flowing,[c] the child's father at once cried out, "I do believe! Help my unbelief!"

Matthew 28:16-17 [16] The eleven disciples went into Galilee to the hillside to which Jesus had directed them. [17] When they saw him, they worshipped him, though some had doubts.

Hebrews 11:1-2 Now faith is the assurance that what we hope for will come about[a] and the certainty that what we cannot see exists. [b] [2] By faith our ancestors won approval.

Hebrews 11:6 [6] Now without faith it is impossible to please God, for whoever comes to him must believe that he exists and that he rewards those who diligently search for him.

Isaiah 55:10-11 "For just as the rain and snow come down from heaven, and do not return there without watering the earth, making it bring forth and sprout, yielding seed for the sower and bread for eating, [11] so will my message be that goes out of my mouth—it won't return to me empty. Instead, it will accomplish what I desire, and achieve the purpose for which I sent it.

Isaiah 59:1 "See, the Lord's hand is not too short to save, nor are his ears[a] too dull to hear.

Romans 4:18-21 [18] Hoping in spite of hopeless circumstances, he believed that he would become "the father of many nations,"[a] just as he had been told:[b] "This is how many descendants you will have."[c] [19] His faith did not weaken when he thought about his own body (which was already[d] as good as dead now that he was about a hundred years old) or about Sarah's inability to have children, [20] nor did he doubt God's promise out of a lack of faith. Instead, his faith became stronger, and he gave glory to God, [21] being absolutely convinced that God would do what he had promised.

Mark 11:22-24 [22] Jesus told his disciples,[a] "Have faith in God! [23] I tell all of you[b] with certainty, if anyone says to this mountain, 'Be lifted up and thrown into the sea,' if he doesn't doubt in his heart but believes that what he says will happen, it will be done for him. [24] That is why I tell you, whatever you ask for in prayer, believe that you have received[c] it and it will be yours.

WHEN YOU ARE PHYSICALLY SICK

Jeremiah 17:14 Heal me, Lord, and I'll be healed; deliver me, and I'll be delivered, because you are my praise.

Jeremiah 30:17 Indeed, I'll bring you healing, and I'll heal you of your wounds,' declares the Lord, 'because they have called you an outcast and have said,[a] "It is Zion, no one cares for her!"'"

Psalm 41:3-4 The Lord will uphold him even on his sickbed; you will transform his bed of illness into health. 4 As for me, I said, "Lord, be gracious to me! Heal me, for I have sinned against you!"

2 Corinthians 4:16-17 16 That's why we are not discouraged. No, even if outwardly we are wearing out, inwardly we are being renewed each and every day. 17 This light, temporary nature of our suffering is producing for us an everlasting weight of glory, far beyond any comparison,

Psalm 103:2-5 Bless the Lord, my soul, and never forget any of his benefits: 3 He continues to forgive all your sins, he continues to heal all your diseases, 4 he continues to redeem your life from the Pit, and he continuously surrounds you with gracious love and compassion. 5 He keeps satisfying you with good things, and he keeps renewing your youth like the eagle's.

James 5:14-15 14 Is anyone among you sick? He should call for the elders of the church, and they should pray for him and anoint him with oil in the name of the Lord. 15 And the prayer offered in faith[a] will save the person who is sick. The Lord will raise him up, and if he has committed any sins, he will be forgiven.

Hebrews 4:16 Let us then with confidence draw near to the throne of grace, that we may receive mercy and find grace to help in time of need.

WHEN YOU ARE IN FINANCIAL TROUBLE

Psalm 23:1 The Lord is the one who is shepherding me; I lack nothing.

1 Timothy 6:9-10 [9] But people who want to get rich keep toppling into temptation and are trapped by many stupid and harmful desires that plunge them into destruction and ruin. [10] For the love of money is a root of all kinds of evil. Some people, in their eagerness to get rich, have wandered away from the faith and caused[a] themselves a lot of pain.

Psalm 37:25 I once was young and now I am old, but I have not seen a righteous person forsaken or his descendants begging for bread.

Malachi 3:10-11 [10] "Bring the entire tithe into the storehouse that there may be food in my house. So put me to the test in this right now," says the Lord of the Heavenly Armies, "and see if I won't throw open the windows[a] of heaven for you and pour out on you blessing without measure. [11] And I'll prevent the devourer from harming you,[b] so that he does not destroy the crops of your land. Nor will the vines in your fields drop their fruit," says the Lord of the Heavenly Armies.

Luke 6:38 [38] Give, and it will be given to you. A large quantity, pressed together, shaken down, and running over will be put into your lap, because you'll be evaluated by the same standard with which you evaluate others."

Romans 13:7 Pay to all what is owed to them: taxes to whom taxes are owed, revenue to whom revenue is owed, respect to whom respect is owed, honor to whom honor is owed.

2 Corinthians 9:6-8 The point is this: whoever sows sparingly will also reap sparingly, and whoever sows bountifully will also reap bountifully. Each one must give as he has decided in his heart, not reluctantly or under compulsion, for God loves a cheerful giver. And God is able to make all grace abound to you, so that having all sufficiency in all things at all times, you may abound in every good work.

2 Corinthians 8:13-15 For I do not mean that others should be eased, and you burdened, but that as a matter of fairness your abundance at the present time should supply their need, so that their abundance may supply your need, that there may be fairness. As it is written, "Whoever gathered much had nothing left over, and whoever gathered little had no lack."

Philippians 4:12-13 "I know what it is to be in need, and I know what it is to have plenty. I have learned the secret of being content in any and every situation, whether well fed or hungry, whether living in plenty or in want. I can do all this through him who gives me strength."

WHAT TO DO TO AVOID MARITAL PROBLEMS

Ephesians 4:26-32 [26] "Be angry, yet do not sin."[a] Do not let the sun set while you are still angry, [27] and do not give the Devil an opportunity to work.[b] [28] The thief must no longer steal but must work hard and do what is good with his own hands, so that he might earn something to give to the needy.

[29] Let no filthy talk be heard from your mouths, but only what is good for building up people and meeting the need of the moment.[c] This way you will administer grace to those who hear you. [30] Do not grieve the Holy Spirit, by whom you were marked with a seal for the day of redemption. [31] Let all bitterness, wrath, anger, quarreling, and slander be put away from you, along with all hatred. [32] And be kind to one another, compassionate, forgiving one another just as God has forgiven you[d] in the Messiah.[e]

Ephesians 5:22-33 [22] Wives, submit yourselves[c] to your husbands as to the Lord. [23] For the husband is the head of his wife as the Messiah[d] is the head of the church. It is he who is the Savior of the body. [24] Indeed, just as the church is submissive to the Messiah,[e] so wives must be submissive[f] to their husbands in everything.

[25] Husbands, love your wives as the Messiah[g] loved the church and gave himself for it, [26] so that he might make it holy by cleansing it, washing it with water and the word, [27] and might present the church to himself in all its glory, without a spot or wrinkle or anything of the kind, but holy and without fault. [28] In the same way, husbands must love their wives as they love[h] their own bodies. A man who loves his wife loves himself. [29] For no one has ever hated his own body, but he nourishes and tenderly cares for it, as the Messiah[i] does[j] the church.

[30] For we are parts of his body—of his flesh and of his bones.[k] [31] "That is why a man will leave his father and mother and be united with his wife, and the two will become one flesh."[l] [32] This is a great secret, but I am talking about the Messiah[m] and the church. [33] But each individual man among you must love his wife as

he loves[n] himself; and may the wife fear her husband.

1 Peter 3:1-15 In a similar way, you wives must submit yourselves to your husbands so that, even if some of them refuse to obey the word, they may be won over without a word through your conduct as wives ²when they see your pure and reverent lives. ³Your beauty should not be an external one, consisting of braided hair or the wearing of gold ornaments and dresses. ⁴Instead, it should be the inner disposition of the heart, consisting in the imperishable quality of a gentle and quiet spirit, which God values greatly.[a] ⁵After all, this is how holy women who set their hope on God used to make themselves beautiful in the past. They submitted themselves to their husbands, ⁶just as Sarah obeyed Abraham and called him lord. You have become her daughters by doing good and by not letting anything terrify you. ⁷In a similar way, you husbands must live with your wives in an understanding manner, as with a most delicate partner.[b] Honor them as heirs with you of the gracious gift of life, so that nothing may interfere with your prayers.

1 Peter 1:22 ²²Now that you have obeyed the truth[a] and have purified your souls to love your brothers sincerely, you must love one another intensely and with a pure heart.

Proverbs 3:5-6 Trust in the Lord with all your heart, and do not depend on your own understanding. ⁶In all your ways acknowledge[a] him, and he will make your paths straight.

Proverbs 10:12 Hatred awakens contention, but love covers all transgressions.

1 Corinthians 16:14 ¹⁴Everything you do should be done lovingly.

Hebrews 13:4 ⁴Let marriage be kept honorable in every way, and the marriage bed undefiled. For God will judge those who commit sexual sins, especially those who commit adultery.

1 Corinthians 7:3-5 ³A husband should fulfill his obligation to his wife, and a wife should do the same for her husband. ⁴A wife does not have authority over her own body, but her husband does. In the same way, a husband doesn't have authority over his own body, but his wife does. [5] Do not withhold yourselves from each other unless you agree to do so just for a set time, in order to devote yourselves to prayer.[a] Then you should come together again so that Satan does not tempt you through your lack of self-control.

1 Corinthians 13:4-8 Love is always patient; love is always kind; love is never envious or arrogant with pride. Love is not conceited, [5] Love is never rude; she never thinks just of herself or ever gets annoyed. Love never is resentful; [6] is never glad with sin; is always glad to side with truth, and pleased that truth will win.[a] [7] Love bears all things, believes all things, hopes all things. Love never fails.

Luke 7:47 [47] So I'm telling you that her sins, as many as they are, have been forgiven, and that's why she has shown such great love. But the one to whom little is forgiven loves little."

Isaiah 43:2 When you pass through the waters, I'll be with you; and through the rivers, they won't sweep over you. when you walk through fire you won't be scorched, and the flame won't set you ablaze.

Proverbs 13:10 Arrogance only brings quarreling, but those receiving advice are wise.

2 Corinthians 10:3-5 [3] Of course, we are living in the world,[a] but we do not wage war in a world-like[b] way. [4] For the weapons of our warfare are not those of the world.[c] Instead, they have the power of God to demolish fortresses. We tear down arguments [5] and every proud obstacle that is raised against the knowledge of God, taking every thought captive in order to obey the Messiah.[d]

1 Peter 4:8 [8] Above all, continue to love each other deeply, because love covers a multitude of sins.

WHAT TO DO WHEN YOU ARE DESERTED BY LOVED ONES

Psalm 9:10 Those who know your name will trust you, for you have not forsaken those who seek you, Lord.

Isaiah 40:11 Like a shepherd, he tends his flock. He gathers the lambs in his arms, carries them close to his heart, and gently leads the mother sheep."

Psalm 27:10 For my father and my mother have forsaken me, but the Lord will take me in.

Psalm 34:17-20 When the righteous cry for help, the Lord hears and delivers them out of all their troubles. The Lord is near to the brokenhearted and saves the crushed in spirit. Many are the afflictions of the righteous, but the Lord delivers him out of them all. He keeps all his bones; not one of them is broken.

Isaiah 49:15-16 "Can a woman forget her nursing child, that she should have no compassion on the son of her womb? Even these may forget, yet I will not forget you. Behold, I have engraved you on the palms of my hands; your walls are continually before me.

Deuteronomy 4:31 [31] For God is compassionate. The Lord your God won't fail you. He won't destroy you or forget the covenant that he confirmed with your ancestors."

Deuteronomy 31:6 [6] Be strong and courageous. Don't fear or tremble before them, because the Lord your God will be the one who keeps on walking with you—he won't leave you or abandon you."

2 Corinthians 4:8-12, 16-18 We are afflicted in every way, but not crushed; perplexed, but not driven to despair; persecuted, but not forsaken; struck down, but not destroyed.

1 John 3:1 See what kind of love the Father has given to us, that we should be called children of God; and so we are. The reason why the world does not know us is that it did not know him.

2 Timothy 4:16 At my first defense no one came to stand by me, but all deserted me. May it not be charged against them!

Psalm 69:8 I have become a stranger to my brothers, an alien to my mother's sons.

Mark 14:50 [50] And His disciples all left Him and fled.

Luke 23:34 Then Jesus said, "Father, forgive them; for they don't know what they're doing."

WHEN YOU DO NOT UNDERSTAND GOD'S WAYS

Isaiah 55:6-9 "Seek the Lord while he[a] may be found, call upon him while he is near.
[7] Let the wicked forsake his way, and the unrighteous person his thoughts. Let him return to the Lord, so he'll have mercy upon him, and to our God, for he'll pardon abundantly.
[8] For my thoughts are not your thoughts, nor are your ways my ways," declares the Lord.

[9] "For just as[b] the heavens are higher than the earth, so are my ways higher than your ways, and my thoughts than your thoughts.

Jeremiah 33:3 [3] 'Call to me and I'll answer you, and will tell you about great and hidden[a] things that you don't know.

1 Corinthians 2:11 For who among men knows the thoughts of a man except the spirit of the man which is in him? Even so the thoughts of God no one knows except the Spirit of God.

Isaiah 41:10 Don't be afraid, because I'm with you; don't be anxious, because I am your God. I keep on strengthening you; I'm truly helping you. I'm surely upholding you with my victorious right hand."

Hosea 6:3 Let us know, let us pursue knowledge of the Lord; his coming is as certain as the dawn. He will come to us like the rain, like the autumn and spring rains come on the earth.

Hebrews 10:23 [23] Let us continue to hold firmly to the hope that we confess without wavering, for the one who made the promise is faithful.

Jeremiah 32:40 [40] I'll make an everlasting covenant with them that I won't turn away from doing good for them. I'll put the fear of me in their hearts, so they won't turn away from me.

Psalm 138:8 The Lord will complete what his purpose is for me. Lord, your gracious love is eternal; do not abandon your personal work in me.

Luke 11:9-10 [9] So I say to you: Keep asking, and it will be given you. Keep searching, and you will find. Keep knocking, and the door[a] will be opened for you, [10] because everyone who keeps asking will receive, and the person who keeps searching will find, and the person who keeps knocking will have the door opened.

Deuteronomy 29:29 [29] "The secret things belong to the Lord our God, but what has been revealed belongs to us and to our children forever, so that we might observe the words of this Law."

Ecclesiastes 3:11 He has made everything appropriate in its time. He has also set eternity in their heart, yet so that man will not find out the work which God has done from the beginning even to the end.

1 Corinthians 2:16 For who has known the mind of the Lord, that he will instruct Him? But we have the mind of Christ

I NEED CONFIDENCE!

2 Corinthians 3:4-5 Such is the confidence that we have through Christ toward God. Not that we are sufficient in ourselves to claim anything as coming from us, but our sufficiency is from God,

Philippians 4:13 [13] I can do all things through him[a] who strengthens me.

Hebrews 13:6 [6] Hence we can confidently say, "The Lord is my helper; I will not be afraid. What can anyone do to me?"

Hebrews 10:35-36 [35] So don't lose your confidence, since it holds a great reward for you. [36] For you need endurance, so that after you have done God's will, you can then receive what he has promised.

Philippians 1:6 [6] being confident of this very thing, that he which hath begun a good work in you will perform *it* until the day of Jesus Christ:

Romans 8:26-27 [26] Now in the same way the Spirit also helps our weakness; for we do not know what to pray for as we should, but the Spirit Himself intercedes for *us* with [a]groanings too deep for words; [27] and He who searches the hearts knows what the mind of the Spirit is, because He intercedes for the [b]saints according to *the will of* God.

Isaiah 40:29-31 He gives power to the weary, and to him who has no might he increases strength. Even youths shall faint and be weary, and young men shall fall exhausted; but they who wait for the Lord shall renew their strength; they shall mount up with wings like eagles; they shall run and not be weary; they shall walk and not faint.

Zechariah 4:6 [6] Then he said to [a]me, "This is the word of the Lord to Zerubbabel, saying, 'Not by might nor by power, but by My Spirit,' says the Lord of armies.

Isaiah 43:2 When you pass through the waters, I will be with you; And through the rivers, they will not overflow you. When you walk through the fire, you will not be scorched, Nor will the flame burn you.

Proverbs 3:26 For the Lord will be [a]your confidence,
And will keep your foot from being caught.

Isaiah 41:10 Fear not, for I am with you; be not dismayed, for I am your God; I will strengthen you, I will help you, I will uphold you with my righteous right hand

2 Corinthians 12:9-10 But he said to me, "My grace is sufficient for you, for my power is made perfect in weakness." Therefore, I will boast all the more gladly of my weaknesses, so that the power of Christ may rest upon me. For the sake of Christ, then, I am content with weaknesses, insults, hardships, persecutions, and calamities. For when I am weak, then I am strong.

WHEN TROUBLES
SEEM TO BE OVERWHELMING

2 Corinthians 4:8-10 *we are* afflicted in every way, but
not crushed; perplexed, but not despairing; [9] persecuted, but
not abandoned; struck down, but not destroyed; [10] always carrying
around in the body the dying of Jesus, so that the life of Jesus may
also be revealed in our body.

Romans 8:35-37 Who shall separate us from the love of Christ? Shall
tribulation, or distress, or persecution, or famine, or nakedness, or
danger, or sword? As it is written, "For your sake we are being killed
all day long; we are regarded as sheep to be slaughtered." No, in all
these things we are more than conquerors through him who loved us.

2 Corinthians 4:16-17 So we do not lose heart. Though our outer
self is wasting away, our inner self is being renewed day by day. For
this light momentary affliction is preparing for us an eternal weight of
glory beyond all comparison,

John 14:1 "Let not your hearts be troubled. Believe in God; believe
also in me.

Isaiah 26:3 You keep him in perfect peace whose mind is stayed on
you, because he trusts in you.

John 14:27-28 Peace I leave with you; my peace I give to you. Not
as the world gives do I give to you. Let not your hearts be troubled,
neither let them be afraid. You heard me say to you, 'I am going away,
and I will come to you.' If you loved me, you would have rejoiced,
because I am going to the Father, for the Father is greater than I.

John 16:22-23 So also you have sorrow now, but I will see you again,
and your hearts will rejoice, and no one will take your joy from
you. In that day you will ask nothing of me. Truly, truly, I say to you,
whatever you ask of the Father in my name, he will give it to you.

James 1:2-4 Count it all joy, my brothers, when you meet trials of
various kinds, for you know that the testing of your faith produces

steadfastness. And let steadfastness have its full effect, that you may be perfect and complete, lacking in nothing.

2 Corinthians 12:10 For the sake of Christ, then, I am content with weaknesses, insults, hardships, persecutions, and calamities. For when I am weak, then I am strong.

1 Peter 1:6-7 In this you rejoice, though now for a little while, if necessary, you have been grieved by various trials, so that the tested genuineness of your faith—more precious than gold that perishes though it is tested by fire—may be found to result in praise and glory and honor at the revelation of Jesus Christ.

Isaiah 43:1-2 But now thus says the Lord, he who created you, O Jacob, he who formed you, O Israel: "Fear not, for I have redeemed you; I have called you by name, you are mine. When you pass through the waters, I will be with you; and through the rivers, they shall not overwhelm you; when you walk through fire you shall not be burned, and the flame shall not consume you.

Romans 5:3-5 More than that, we rejoice in our sufferings, knowing that suffering produces endurance, and endurance produces character, and character produces hope, and hope does not put us to shame, because God's love has been poured into our hearts through the Holy Spirit who has been given to us.

Psalm 42:5 Why are you cast down, O my soul, and why are you in turmoil within me? Hope in God; for I shall again praise him, my salvation and my God.

WHAT THE
BIBLE SAYS ABOUT FAITH

Hebrews 11:3 By faith we understand that the universe was created by the word of God, so that what is seen was not made out of things that are visible.

Romans 10:17 So faith comes from hearing and hearing through the word of Christ.

Matthew 17:20 He said to them, "Because of your little faith. For truly, I say to you, if you have faith like a grain of mustard seed, you will say to this mountain, 'Move from here to there,' and it will move, and nothing will be impossible for you."

Luke 1:37 For nothing will be impossible with God."

Matthew 21:21 And Jesus answered them, "Truly, I say to you, if you have faith and do not doubt, you will not only do what has been done to the fig tree, but even if you say to this mountain, 'Be taken up and thrown into the sea,' it will happen.

Mark 9:23-24 [23] But Jesus said to him, "'If You can?' All things are possible for the one who believes." [24] Immediately the boy's father cried out and said, "I do believe; help my unbelief!"

Romans 1:17 [17] For in it the righteousness of God is revealed [a]from faith to faith; as it is written: "[b]But the righteous *one* will live by faith."

2 Corinthians 5:7 We live by what we believe, not by what we can see.

Hebrews 11:6 [6] And without faith it is impossible to please Him, for the one who comes to God must believe that He exists, and that He proves to be One who rewards those who seek Him.

1 Peter 1:7-9 [7] so that the [a]proof of your faith, *being* more precious than gold which perishes though tested by fire, may be found to result in praise, glory, and honor at the revelation of Jesus

Christ; **⁸** and though you have not seen Him, you love Him, and though you do not see Him now, but believe in Him, you greatly rejoice with joy inexpressible and [b]full of glory, **⁹** obtaining as the outcome of your faith, the salvation of [c]your souls.

1 John 5:3-5 **³** Loving God means obeying his commands. And God's commands are not too hard for us, **⁴** because everyone who is a child of God conquers the world. And this is the victory that conquers the world—our faith. **⁵** So the one who conquers the world is the person who believes that Jesus is the Son of God.

Matthew 9:20-22 **²⁰** Then a woman who had been bleeding for twelve years came behind Jesus and touched the edge of his coat. **²¹** She was thinking, "If I can just touch his clothes, I will be healed." **²²** Jesus turned and saw the woman and said, "Be encouraged, dear woman. You are made well because you believed." And the woman was healed from that moment on.

LOVE – THE LAW WRAPPED INTO ONE WORD

Mark 12:30-31 [30] Love the Lord your God with all your heart, all your soul, all your mind, and all your strength.'[a] [31] The second command is this: 'Love your neighbor as you love yourself.'[b] There are no commands more important than these."

1 John 4:10-12 [10] This is what real love is: It is not our love for God; it is God's love for us. He sent his Son to die in our place to take away our sins. [11] Dear friends, if God loved us that much we also should love each other. [12] No one has ever seen God, but if we love each other, God lives in us, and his love is made perfect in us.

John 15:12-14, 17 [12] "This is my command: Love each other as I have loved you. [13] The greatest love a person can show is to die for his friends. [14] You are my friends if you do what I command you. [17] This is my command: Love each other.

1 John 4:7-8 [7] Dear friends, we should love each other, because love comes from God. Everyone who loves has become God's child and knows God. [8] Whoever does not love does not know God, because God is love.

1 Corinthians 13:1-8, 13 I may speak in different languages[a] of people or even angels. But if I do not have love, I am only a noisy bell or a crashing cymbal. [2] I may have the gift of prophecy. I may understand all the secret things of God and have all knowledge, and I may have faith so great I can move mountains. But even with all these things, if I do not have love, then I am nothing. [3] I may give away everything I have, and I may even give my body as an offering to be burned.[b] But I gain nothing if I do not have love.

[4] Love is patient and kind. Love is not jealous, it does not brag, and it is not proud. [5] Love is not rude, is not selfish, and does not get upset with others. Love does not count up wrongs that have been done. [6] Love takes no pleasure in evil but rejoices over the truth. [7] Love patiently accepts all things. It always trusts, always

hopes, and always endures. **8** Love never ends. **13** So these three things continue forever: faith, hope, and love. And the greatest of these is love.

John 15:9-10 **9** I loved you as the Father loved me. Now remain in my love. **10** I have obeyed my Father's commands, and I remain in his love. In the same way, if you obey my commands, you will remain in my love.

John 14:21 **21** Those who know my commands and obey them are the ones who love me, and my Father will love those who love me. I will love them and will show myself to them."

John 13:34-35 **34** "I give you a new command: Love each other. You must love each other as I have loved you. **35** All people will know that you are my followers if you love each other."

1 John 4:16, 19-21 **16** And so we know the love that God has for us, and we trust that love. God is love. Those who live in love live in God, and God lives in them. **19** We love because God first loved us. **20** If people say, "I love God," but hate their brothers or sisters, they are liars. Those who do not love their brothers and sisters, whom they have seen, cannot love God, whom they have never seen.

Jeremiah 31:3 **3** And from far away the Lord appeared to his people and said, "I love you people with a love that will last forever. That is why I have continued showing you kindness."

John 16:27 **27** The Father himself loves you. He loves you because you loved me and believed that I came from God.

Romans 8:37-39 **37** But in all these things we are completely victorious through God who showed his love for us. **38** Yes, I am sure that neither death, nor life, nor angels, nor ruling spirits, nothing now, nothing in the future, no powers, **39** nothing above us, nothing below us, nor anything else in the whole world will ever be able to separate us from the love of God that is in Christ Jesus our Lord.

Romans 5:8 ⁸ But God shows his great love for us in this way: Christ died for us while we were still sinners.

John 3:16 ¹⁶ "God loved the world so much that he gave his one and only Son so that whoever believes in him may not be lost but have eternal life.

WHAT THE
BIBLE SAYS ABOUT DEATH

2 Samuel 14:14 [14] We will all die someday. We're like water spilled on the ground; no one can gather it back. But God doesn't take away life. Instead, he plans ways that those who have been sent away will not have to stay away from him!

Psalm 49:10-15 See, even wise people die. Fools and stupid people also die and leave their wealth to others. [11] Their graves will always be their homes. They will live there from now on, even though they named places after themselves. [12] Even rich people do not live forever; like the animals, people die. [13] This is what will happen to those who trust in themselves and to their followers who believe them. [14] Like sheep, they must die, and death will be their shepherd. Honest people will rule over them in the morning, and their bodies will rot in a grave far from home. [15] But God will save my life and will take me from the grave.

John 8:23-24 [23] Jesus said, "You people are from here below, but I am from above. You belong to this world, but I don't belong to this world. [24] So I told you that you would die in your sins. Yes, you will die in your sins if you don't believe that I am he."

Colossians 2:12-13 [12] When you were baptized, you were buried with Christ, and you were raised up with him through your faith in God's power that was shown when he raised Christ from the dead. [13] When you were spiritually dead because of your sins and because you were not free from the power of your sinful self,

John 8:51 [51] I tell you the truth, whoever obeys my teaching will never die."

John 11:25 Jesus said to her, "I am the resurrection and the life. Those who believe in me will have life even if they die.

2 Timothy 1:10 [10] but it is now shown to us by the coming of our Savior Christ Jesus. He destroyed death, and through the Good News he showed us the way to have life that cannot be destroyed.

Proverbs 14:27, 32 Respect for the Lord gives life. It is like a fountain that can save people from death. The wicked are ruined by their own evil, but those who do right are protected even in death.

Romans 14:8-9 [8] If we live, we are living for the Lord, and if we die, we are dying for the Lord. So, living or dying, we belong to the Lord.

[9] The reason Christ died and rose from the dead to live again was so he would be Lord over both the dead and the living.

John 5:21, 24 [21] Just as the Father raises the dead and gives them life, so also the Son gives life to those he wants to. [24] "I tell you the truth, whoever hears what I say and believes in the One who sent me has eternal life. That person will not be judged guilty but has already left

d

WHAT THE BIBLE SAYS ABOUT ETERNITY

John 6:46-47 [46] No one has seen the Father except the One who is from God; only he has seen the Father. [47] I tell you the truth, whoever believes has eternal life.

Psalm 49:15 But God will save my life and will take me from the grave.

John 3:16-18 [16] "God loved the world so much that he gave his one and only Son so that whoever believes in him may not be lost but have eternal life. [17] God did not send his Son into the world to judge the world guilty, but to save the world through him. [18] People who believe in God's Son are not judged guilty. Those who do not believe have already been judged guilty, because they have not believed in God's one and only Son.

John 5:24 [24] "I tell you the truth, whoever hears what I say and believes in the One who sent me has eternal life. That person will not be judged guilty but has already left death and entered life.

1 John 5:11-12 [11] This is what God told us: God has given us eternal life, and this life is in his Son. [12] Whoever has the Son has life, but whoever does not have the Son of God does not have life.

Psalm 23:6 Surely your goodness and love will be with me all my life, and I will live in the house of the Lord forever.

Psalm 37:18 The Lord watches over the lives of the innocent, and their reward will last forever.

John 6:50-51 [50] Here is the bread that comes down from heaven. Anyone who eats this bread will never die. [51] I am the living bread that came down from heaven. Anyone who eats this bread will live forever. This bread is my flesh, which I will give up so that the world may have life."

1 Corinthians 15:54-57 [54] So this body that can be destroyed will clothe itself with that which can never be destroyed, and this body that dies will clothe itself with that which can never die. When this happens, this Scripture will be made true:

"Death is destroyed forever in victory." [55] "Death, where is your victory? Death, where is your pain?"

[56] Death's power to hurt is sin, and the power of sin is the law. [57] But we thank God! He gives us the victory through our Lord Jesus Christ.

John 4:13-14 [13] Jesus answered, "Everyone who drinks this water will be thirsty again, [14] but whoever drinks the water I give will never be thirsty. The water I give will become a spring of water gushing up inside that person, giving eternal life."

1 John 5:20 [20] We also know that the Son of God has come and has given us understanding so that we can know the True One. And our lives are in the True One and in his Son, Jesus Christ. He is the true God and the eternal life.

John 11:25-26 [25] Jesus said to her, "I am the resurrection and the life. Those who believe in me will have life even if they die. [26] And everyone who lives and believes in me will never die. Martha, do you believe this?"

John 6:27 [27] Don't work for the food that spoils. Work for the food that stays good always and gives eternal life. The Son of Man will give you this food, because on him God the Father has put his power."

John 10:27-28 [27] My sheep listen to my voice; I know them, and they follow me. [28] I give them eternal life, and they will never die, and no one can steal them out of my hand.

WHAT THE
BIBLE SAYS ABOUT PRAISE

Hebrews 12:28-29 [24] "I tell you the truth, whoever hears what I say and believes in the One who sent me has eternal life. That person will not be judged guilty but has already left death and entered life.

Hebrews 13:15-16 Through Jesus, therefore, let us continually offer to God a sacrifice of praise — the fruit of lips that openly profess his name. And do not forget to do good and to share with others, for with such sacrifices God is pleased.

Colossians 3:15-17 [15] Let the peace that Christ gives control your thinking, because you were all called together in one body[a] to have peace. Always be thankful. [16] Let the teaching of Christ live in you richly. Use all wisdom to teach and instruct each other by singing psalms, hymns, and spiritual songs with thankfulness in your hearts to God. [17] Everything you do or say should be done to obey Jesus your Lord. And in all you do, give thanks to God the Father through Jesus.

1 Peter 2:9 [9] But you are a chosen people, royal priests, a holy nation, a people for God's own possession. You were chosen to tell about the wonderful acts of God, who called you out of darkness into his wonderful light.

Psalm 147:1 It is good to sing praises to our God; it is good and pleasant to praise him.

2 Samuel 22:4 It is good to sing praises to our God; it is good and pleasant to praise him.

Psalm 34:1-3 I will praise the Lord at all times; his praise is always on my lips. [2] My whole being praises the Lord. The poor will hear and be glad. [3] Glorify the Lord with me and let us praise his name together.

Psalm 107:8 Let them give thanks to the Lord for his love and for the miracles he does for people.

Ephesians 5:18-20 [18] Do not be drunk with wine, which will ruin you, but be filled with the Spirit. [19] Speak to each other with psalms, hymns, and spiritual songs, singing and making music in your hearts to the Lord. [20] Always give thanks to God the Father for everything, in the name of our Lord Jesus Christ.

Psalm 47:1-2, 6-7 Clap your hands, all you people. Shout to God with joy. [2] The Lord Most High is wonderful.   Sing praises to God. Sing praises. Sing praises to our King. Sing praises.   [7] God is King of all the earth, so sing a song of praise to him.

Psalm 50:23 Those people honor me who bring me offerings to show thanks.

And I, God, will save those who do that."

Psalm 63:3-5 Because your love is better than life, I will praise you. [4] I will praise you as long as I live. I will lift up my hands in prayer to your name. [5] I will be content as if I had eaten the best foods. My lips will sing, and my mouth will praise you.

Psalm 71:5-8 Lord, you are my hope. Lord, I have trusted you since I was young. [6] I have depended on you since I was born; you helped me even on the day of my birth. I will always praise you. [7] I am an example to many people, because you are my strong protection. [8] I am always praising you; all day long I honor you.

Psalm 92:1-5 It is good to praise you, Lord, to sing praises to God Most High. [2] It is good to tell of your love in the morning and of your loyalty at night. [3] It is good to praise you with the ten-stringed lyre and with the soft-sounding harp. [4] Lord, you have made me happy by what you have done; I will sing for joy about what your hands have done. [5] Lord, you have done such great things! How deep are your thoughts!

Psalm 96:4-8 because the Lord is great; he should be praised at all times. He should be honored more than all the gods, [5] because all the gods of the nations are only idols, but the Lord made the heavens. [6] The Lord has glory and majesty; he has power and beauty in his Temple. [7] Praise the Lord, all nations on earth; praise the Lord's glory and power. ⁸ Praise the glory of the Lord's name. Bring an offering and come into his Temple courtyards.

Acts 16:25 ²⁵ About midnight Paul and Silas were praying and singing songs to God as the other prisoners listened.

SERVING GOD

Colossians 3:23 Whatever you do, do your work heartily, as for the Lord rather than for men

Exodus 23:25 But you shall serve the Lord your God, and He will bless your bread and your water; and I will remove sickness from your midst.

Romans 1:9 For God, whom I serve in my spirit in the preaching of the gospel of His Son, is my witness as to how unceasingly I make mention of you,

1 Samuel 12:20 Samuel said to the people, "Do not fear. You have committed all this evil, yet do not turn aside from following the Lord, but serve the Lord with all your heart.

Romans 7:25 Thanks be to God through Jesus Christ our Lord! So then, on the one hand I myself with my mind am serving the law of God, but on the other, with my flesh the law of sin.

Luke 16:13 No servant can serve two masters; for either he will hate the one and love the other, or else he will be devoted to one and despise the other. You cannot serve God and wealth."

Romans 7:6 ⁶In the past, the law held us like prisoners, but our old selves died, and we were made free from the law. So now we serve God in a new way with the Spirit, and not in the old way with written rules.

Galatians 1:10 For am I now seeking the favor of men, or of God? Or am I striving to please men? If I were still trying to please men, I would not be a bond-servant of Christ.

1 Samuel 12:24 Only fear the Lord and serve Him in truth with all your heart; for consider what great things He has done for you.

Joshua 24:14 "Now, therefore, fear the Lord and serve Him in sincerity and truth; and put away the gods which your fathers served beyond the River and in Egypt, and serve the Lord.

Romans 12:10-13 [10] Love each other like brothers and sisters. Give each other more honor than you want for yourselves. [11] Do not be lazy but work hard, serving the Lord with all your heart. [12] Be joyful because you have hope. Be patient when trouble comes and pray at all times. [13] Share with God's people who need help. Bring strangers in need into your homes.

Deuteronomy 10:12-13 [12] Now, Israel, this is what the Lord your God wants you to do: Respect the Lord your God and do what he has told you to do. Love him. Serve the Lord your God with your whole being, [13] and obey the Lord's commands and laws that I am giving you today for your own good.

Deuteronomy 11:13-15 [13] If you carefully obey the commands, I am giving you today and love the Lord your God and serve him with your whole being, [14] then he will send rain on your land at the right time, in the fall and spring, and you will be able to gather your grain, new wine, and oil. [15] He will put grass in the fields for your cattle, and you will have plenty to eat.

Joshua 24:15 [15] But if you don't want to serve the Lord, you must choose for yourselves today whom you will serve. You may serve the gods that your ancestors worshiped when they lived on the other side of the Euphrates River, or you may serve the gods of the Amorites who lived in this land. As for me and my family, we will serve the Lord."

1 Samuel 12:20-22 [20] Samuel answered, "Don't be afraid. It's true that you did wrong, but don't turn away from the Lord. Serve the Lord with all your heart. [21] Idols are of no use, so don't worship them. They can't help you or save you. They are useless! [22] For his own sake, the Lord won't leave his people. Instead, he was pleased to make you his own people.

1 Chronicles 28:9 [9] "And you, my son Solomon, accept the God of your father. Serve him completely and willingly, because the Lord knows what is in everyone's mind. He understands everything you think. If you go to him for help, you will get an answer. But if you turn away from him, he will leave you forever.

Job 36:11 "If they hear and serve Him, they will end their days in prosperity And their years in pleasures.

BEING
OBEDIENT TO THE LORD

Deuteronomy 11:26-28 [26] See, today I am letting you choose a blessing or a curse. [27] You will be blessed if you obey the commands of the Lord your God that I am giving you today. [28] But you will be cursed if you disobey the commands of the Lord your God. So do not disobey the commands I am giving you today, and do not worship other gods you do not know.

Deuteronomy 5:1, 32-33 Moses called all the people of Israel together and said: Listen, Israel, to the commands and laws I am giving you today. Learn them and obey them carefully.   [32] So be careful to do what the Lord your God has commanded you and follow the commands exactly. [33] Live the way the Lord your God has commanded you so that you may live and have what is good and have a long life in the land you will take.

1 Kings 3:14 If you follow me and obey my laws and commands, as your father David did, I will also give you a long life."

1 Samuel 15:22 But Samuel answered, "What pleases the Lord more: burnt offerings and sacrifices or obedience to his voice? It is better to obey than to sacrifice. It is better to listen to God than to offer the fat of sheep.

Ephesians 6:1-3 Children, obey your parents as the Lord wants, because this is the right thing to do. [2] The command says, "Honor your father and mother."[a] This is the first command that has a promise with it— [3] "Then everything will be well with you, and you will have a long life on the earth."

Colossians 3:20, 22-24 Children, obey your parents in all things, because this pleases the Lord. [22] Slaves, obey your masters in all things. Do not obey just when they are watching you, to gain their favor, but serve them honestly, because you respect the Lord. [23] In all the work you are doing, work the best you can. Work as if you were doing it for the Lord, not for people. [24] Remember that you will receive your reward from the Lord,

Isaiah 48:17-18 This is what the Lord, who saves you, the Holy One of Israel, says: "I am the Lord your God, who teaches you to do what is good, who leads you in the way you should go. ¹⁸ If you had obeyed me, you would have had peace like a full-flowing river. Good things would have flowed to you like the waves of the sea.

Jeremiah 7:23 I also gave them this command: Obey me, and I will be your God and you will be my people. Do all that I command so that good things will happen to you.

John 14:15, 21 ¹⁵ "If you love me, you will obey my commands. ²¹ Those who know my commands and obey them are the ones who love me, and my Father will love those who love me. I will love them and will show myself to them."

Psalm 143:10 Teach me to do what you want, because you are my God. Let your good Spirit lead me on level ground.

1 Peter 2:13-21 ¹³ For the Lord's sake, yield to the people who have authority in this world: the king, who is the highest authority, ¹⁴ and the leaders who are sent by him to punish those who do wrong and to praise those who do right. ¹⁵ It is God's desire that by doing good you should stop foolish people from saying stupid things about you. ¹⁶ Live as free people, but do not use your freedom as an excuse to do evil. Live as servants of God. ¹⁷ Show respect for all people: Love the brothers and sisters of God's family, respect God, honor the king.

¹⁸ Slaves, yield to the authority of your masters with all respect, not only those who are good and kind, but also those who are dishonest. ¹⁹ A person might have to suffer even when it is unfair, but if he thinks of God and can stand the pain, God is pleased. ²⁰ If you are beaten for doing wrong, there is no reason to praise you for being patient in your punishment. But if you suffer for doing good, and you are patient, then God is pleased. ²¹ This is what you were called to do, because Christ suffered for you and gave you an example to follow. So, you should do as he did.

1 John 2:2-6 ² He died in our place to take away our sins, and not only our sins but the sins of all people. [3] We can be sure that we know God if we obey his commands. [4] Anyone who says, "I know God," but does not obey God's commands is a liar, and the truth is not in that person. [5] But if someone obeys God's teaching, then in that person God's love has truly reached its goal. This is how we can be sure we are living in God: [6] Whoever says that he lives in God must live as Jesus lived.

THE WORLDLY MIND

James 4:2-4 ² You want things, but you do not have them. So you are ready to kill and are jealous of other people, but you still cannot get what you want. So you argue and fight. You do not get what you want, because you do not ask God. ³ Or when you ask, you do not receive because the reason you ask is wrong. You want things so you can use them for your own pleasures. ⁴ So, you are not loyal to God! You should know that loving the world is the same as hating God. Anyone who wants to be a friend of the world becomes God's enemy.

Matthew 16:26 ²⁶ It is worthless to have the whole world if they lose their souls. They could never pay enough to buy back their souls.

Matthew 6:24 ²⁴ "No one can serve two masters. The person will hate one master and love the other or will follow one master and refuse to follow the other. You cannot serve both God and worldly riches.

1 John 3:17 ¹⁷ Suppose someone has enough to live and sees a brother or sister in need but does not help. Then God's love is not living in that person.

Romans 8:6-8 ⁶ If people's thinking is controlled by the sinful self, there is death. But if their thinking is controlled by the Spirit, there is life and peace. ⁷ When people's thinking is controlled by the sinful self, they are against God, because they refuse to obey God's law and really are not even able to obey God's law. ⁸ Those people who are ruled by their sinful selves cannot please God.

1 Timothy 6:17 ¹⁷ Command those who are rich with things of this world not to be proud. Tell them to hope in God, not in their uncertain riches. God richly gives us everything to enjoy.

Galatians 6:8-9 ⁸ If they plant to satisfy their sinful selves, their sinful selves will bring them ruin. But if they plant to please the Spirit, they will receive eternal life from the Spirit. ⁹ We must not become tired of doing good. We will receive our harvest of eternal life at the right time if we do not give up.

Proverbs 14:12-14 Some people think they are doing right, but in the end it leads to death. [13] Someone who is laughing may be sad inside, and joy may end in sadness. [14] Evil people will be paid back for their evil ways, and good people will be rewarded for their good ones.

Proverbs 11:28 Those who trust in riches will be ruined, but a good person will be healthy like a green leaf.

Philippians 3:18-21 [18] Many people live like enemies of the cross of Christ. I have often told you about them, and it makes me cry to tell you about them now. [19] In the end, they will be destroyed. They do whatever their bodies want, they are proud of their shameful acts, and they think only about earthly things. [20] But our homeland is in heaven, and we are waiting for our Savior, the Lord Jesus Christ, to come from heaven. [21] By his power to rule all things, he will change our humble bodies and make them like his own glorious body.

2 Timothy 3:1-7 But mark this: There will be terrible times in the last days. [2] People will be lovers of themselves, lovers of money, boastful, proud, abusive, disobedient to their parents, ungrateful, unholy, [3] without love, unforgiving, slanderous, without self-control, brutal, not lovers of the good, [4] treacherous, rash, conceited, lovers of pleasure rather than lovers of God— [5] having a form of godliness but denying its power. Have nothing to do with such people. [6] They are the kind who worm their way into homes and gain control over gullible women, who are loaded down with sins and are swayed by all kinds of evil desires, [7] always learning but never able to come to a knowledge of the truth.

1 Peter 2:11-12 [11] Dear friends, I urge you, as foreigners and exiles, to abstain from sinful desires, which wage war against your soul. [12] Live such good lives among the pagans that, though they accuse you of doing wrong, they may see your good deeds and glorify God on the day he visits us.

1 John 2:15-17 [15] Do not love the world or anything in the world. If anyone loves the world, love for the Father[a] is not in them. [16] For everything in the world—the lust of the flesh, the lust of the eyes, and the pride of life—comes not from the Father but from the world. [17] The world and its desires pass away, but whoever does the will of God lives forever.

Romans 12:1-2, 9 Therefore, I urge you, brothers and sisters, in view of God's mercy, to offer your bodies as a living sacrifice, holy and pleasing to God—this is your true and proper worship. [2] Do not conform to the pattern of this world, but be transformed by the renewing of your mind. Then you will be able to test and approve what God's will is—his good, pleasing and perfect will. [9] Love must be sincere. Hate what is evil; cling to what is good.

Philippians 2:3-5 [3] Do nothing out of selfish ambition or vain conceit. Rather, in humility value others above yourselves, [4] not looking to your own interests but each of you to the interests of the others.

Isaiah 26:3-4 You will keep in perfect peace those whose minds are steadfast, because they trust in you. [4] Trust in the Lord forever, for the Lord, the Lord himself, is the Rock eternal.

Colossians 3:2, 5-6, 8-10 [2] Set your minds on things above, not on earthly things. [5] Put to death, therefore, whatever belongs to your earthly nature: sexual immorality, impurity, lust, evil desires and greed, which is idolatry. [6] Because of these, the wrath of God is coming. [8] But now you must also rid yourselves of all such things as these: anger, rage, malice, slander, and filthy language from your lips. [9] Do not lie to each other, since you have taken off your old self with its practices [10] and have put on the new self, which is being renewed in knowledge in the image of its Creator.

Philippians 4:8 [8] Finally, brothers and sisters, whatever is true, whatever is noble, whatever is right, whatever is pure, whatever is lovely, whatever is admirable—if anything is excellent or praiseworthy—think about such things.

UNACCEPTABLE SEXUAL BEHAVIOR

Romans 1:18-28 [18] The wrath of God is being revealed from heaven against all the godlessness and wickedness of people, who suppress the truth by their wickedness, [19] since what may be known about God is plain to them, because God has made it plain to them. [20] For since the creation of the world God's invisible qualities—his eternal power and divine nature—have been clearly seen, being understood from what has been made, so that people are without excuse. [21] For although they knew God, they neither glorified him as God nor gave thanks to him, but their thinking became futile and their foolish hearts were darkened. [22] Although they claimed to be wise, they became fools [23] and exchanged the glory of the immortal God for images made to look like a mortal human being and birds and animals and reptiles. [24] Therefore God gave them over in the sinful desires of their hearts to sexual impurity for the degrading of their bodies with one another. [25] They exchanged the truth about God for a lie, and worshiped and served created things rather than the Creator—who is forever praised. Amen.

[26] Because of this, God gave them over to shameful lusts. Even their women exchanged natural sexual relations for unnatural ones. [27] In the same way the men also abandoned natural relations with women and were inflamed with lust for one another. Men committed shameful acts with other men, and received in themselves the due penalty for their error. [28] Furthermore, just as they did not think it worthwhile to retain the knowledge of God, so God gave them over to a depraved mind, so that they do what ought not to be done.

1 Thessalonians 4:1-5 As for other matters, brothers and sisters, we instructed you how to live in order to please God, as in fact you are living. Now we ask you and urge you in the Lord Jesus to do this more and more. [2] For you know what instructions we gave you by the authority of the Lord Jesus. [3] It is God's will that you should be sanctified: that you should avoid sexual immorality; [4] that each of you should learn to control your own body[a] in a way that is holy and honorable, ⁵ not in passionate lust like the pagans, who do not know God;

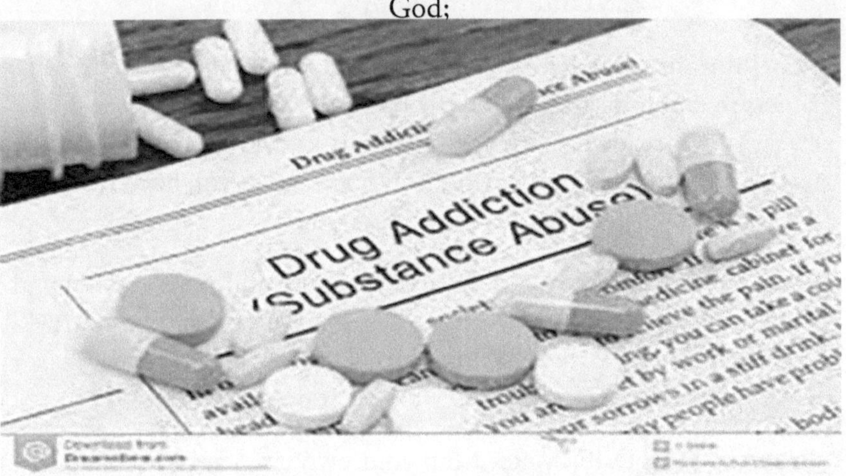

Proverbs 6:20-29 My son, keep your father's command and do not forsake your mother's teaching. ²¹ Bind them always on your heart; fasten them around your neck. ²² When you walk, they will guide you; when you sleep, they will watch over you; when you awake, they will speak to you. ²³ For this command is a lamp, this teaching is a light, and correction and instruction are the way to life, ²⁴ keeping you from your neighbor's wife, from the smooth talk of a wayward woman. ²⁵ Do not lust in your heart after her beauty or let her captivate you with her eyes. ²⁶ For a prostitute can be had for a loaf of bread, but another man's wife preys on your very life. ²⁷ Can a man scoop fire into his lap without his clothes being burned? ²⁸ Can a man walk on hot coals without his feet being scorched? ²⁹ So is he who sleeps with another man's wife; no one who touches her will go unpunished.

Matthew 5:27-28 ²⁷ "You have heard that it was said, 'You shall not commit adultery.'[a] ²⁸ But I tell you that anyone who looks at a woman lustfully has already committed adultery with her in his heart.

1 Corinthians 6:12-13 ¹² "I have the right to do anything," you say—but not everything is beneficial. "I have the right to do anything"—but I will not be mastered by anything. ¹³ You say, "Food for the stomach and the stomach for food, and God will destroy them both." The body, however, is not meant for sexual immorality but for the Lord, and the Lord for the body.

1 Corinthians 6:18-19 [18] Flee from sexual immorality. All other sins a person commits are outside the body, but whoever sins sexually, sins against their own body. [19] Do you not know that your bodies are temples of the Holy Spirit, who is in you, whom you have received from God? You are not your own;

Jeremiah 17:9-10 The heart is deceitful above all things and beyond cure. Who can understand it? [10] "I the Lord search the heart and examine the mind, to reward each person according to their conduct, according to what their deeds deserve."

Proverbs 5:15 Drink water from your own cistern, running water from your own well.

1 John 1:9 If we confess our sins, he is faithful and just and will forgive us our sins and purify us from all unrighteousness.

1 John 2:2 [2] He is the atoning sacrifice for our sins, and not only for

SUBSTANCE ABUSE

1 Corinthians 6:19-20 [19] Do you not know that your bodies are temples of the Holy Spirit, who is in you, whom you have received from God? You are not your own; [20] you were bought at a price. Therefore, honor God with your bodies.

Ephesians 5:18 And do not get drunk with wine, for that is debauchery, but be filled with the Spirit,

Romans 13:12-14 [12] The night is nearly over; the day is almost here. So let us put aside the deeds of darkness and put on the armor of light. [13] Let us behave decently, as in the daytime, not in carousing and drunkenness, not in sexual immorality and debauchery, not in dissension and jealousy. [14] Rather, clothe yourselves with the Lord Jesus Christ, and do not think about how to gratify the desires of the flesh.[a]

1 John 1:8-9 [8] If we claim to be without sin, we deceive ourselves and the truth is not in us. [9] If we confess our sins, he is faithful and just and will forgive us our sins and purify us from all unrighteousness.

John 10:9-10 [9] I am the gate; whoever enters through me will be saved.[a] They will come in and go out, and find pasture. [10] The thief comes only to steal and kill and destroy; I have come that they may have life and have it to the full.

Proverbs 23:19-21, 23 Listen, my son, and be wise, and set your heart on the right path: [20] Do not join those who drink too much wine or gorge themselves on meat, [21] for drunkards and gluttons become poor, and drowsiness clothes them in rags. [23] Buy the truth and do not sell it—wisdom, instruction and insight as well.

1 Peter 5:7-8 [7] Cast all your anxiety on him because he cares for you. [8] Be alert and of sober mind. Your enemy the devil prowls around like a roaring lion looking for someone to devour. [9] Resist him, standing firm in the faith, because you know that the family of believers throughout the world is undergoing the same kind of sufferings.

2 Corinthians 1:3-4 [3] Praise be to the God and Father of our Lord Jesus Christ, the Father of compassion and the God of all comfort, [4] who comforts us in all our troubles, so that we can comfort those in any trouble with the comfort we ourselves receive from God.

THE HOLY SPIRIT

1 Corinthians 6:19 [19] Do you not know that your bodies are temples of the Holy Spirit, who is in you, whom you have received from God? You are not your own;

John 16:7-9, 14 [7] But very truly I tell you, it is for your good that I am going away. Unless I go away, the Advocate will not come to you; but if I go, I will send him to you. [8] When he comes, he will prove the world to be in the wrong about sin and righteousness and judgment: [9] about sin, because people do not believe in me;   [14] He will glorify me because it is from me that he will receive what he will make known to you.

John 7:38-39 [38] Whoever believes in me, as Scripture has said, rivers of living water will flow from within them."[a] [39] By this he meant the Spirit, whom those who believed in him were later to receive. Up to that time the Spirit had not been given, since Jesus had not yet been glorified.

John 14:16-20 [16] And I will ask the Father, and he will give you another advocate to help you and be with you forever— [17] the Spirit of truth. The world cannot accept him, because it neither sees him nor knows him. But you know him, for he lives with you and will be[a] in you. [18] I will not leave you as orphans; I will come to you. [19] Before long, the world will not see me anymore, but you will see me. Because I live, you also will live. [20] On that day you will realize that I am in my Father, and you are in me, and I am in you.

Romans 5:5 [5] And hope does not put us to shame, because God's love has been poured out into our hearts through the Holy Spirit, who has been given to us.

Matthew 3:11 [11] "I baptize you with[a] water for repentance. But after me comes one who is more powerful than I, whose sandals I am not worthy to carry. He will baptize you with[b] the Holy Spirit and fire.

Ephesians 5:18-20 [18] Do not get drunk on wine, which leads to debauchery. Instead, be filled with the Spirit, [19] speaking to one another with psalms, hymns, and songs from the Spirit. Sing and make music from your heart to the Lord, [20] always giving thanks to God the Father for everything, in the name of our Lord Jesus Christ.

Acts 1:4-5, 7-8 [4] On one occasion, while he was eating with them, he gave them this command: "Do not leave Jerusalem, but wait for the gift my Father promised, which you have heard me speak about. [5] For John baptized with[a] water, but in a few days you will be baptized with[b] the Holy Spirit." [7] He said to them: "It is not for you to know the times or dates the Father has set by his own authority. [8] But you will receive power when the Holy Spirit comes on you; and you will be my witnesses in Jerusalem, and in all Judea and Samaria, and to the ends of the earth."

Acts 2:4 [4] All of them were filled with the Holy Spirit and began to speak in other tongues[a] as the Spirit enabled them.

Acts 2:38 [38] Peter replied, "Repent and be baptized, every one of you, in the name of Jesus Christ for the forgiveness of your sins. And you will receive the gift of the Holy Spirit.

Acts 4:31 [31] After they prayed, the place where they were meeting was shaken. And they were all filled with the Holy Spirit and spoke the word of God boldly.

Acts 8:14-17 [14] When the apostles in Jerusalem heard that Samaria had accepted the word of God, they sent Peter and John to Samaria. [15] When they arrived, they prayed for the new believers there that they might receive the Holy Spirit, [16] because the Holy Spirit had not yet come on any of them; they had simply been baptized in the name of the Lord Jesus. [17] Then Peter and John placed their hands on them, and they received the Holy Spirit.

Acts 10:44-47 [44] While Peter was still speaking these words, the Holy Spirit came on all who heard the message. [45] The circumcised believers who had come with Peter were astonished that the gift of the Holy Spirit had been poured out even on Gentiles. [46] For they heard them speaking in tongues[a] and praising God. Then Peter said, [47] "Surely no one can stand in the way of their being baptized with.

GOD'S FAITHFULNESS

Psalm 121:3, 7-8 He will not let your foot slip—he who watches over you will not slumber; The Lord will keep you from all harm—he will watch over your life; [8] the Lord will watch over your coming and going both now and forevermore.

Psalm 89:1-2, 19, 34 I will sing of the Lord's great love forever; with my mouth I will make your faithfulness known through all generations. [2] I will declare that your love stands firm forever, that you have established your faithfulness in heaven itself. I will not violate my covenant or alter what my lips have uttered.

Isaiah 54:9-10 "To me this is like the days of Noah, when I swore that the waters of Noah would never again cover the earth. So now I have sworn not to be angry with you, never to rebuke you again. [10] Though the mountains be shaken, and the hills be removed, yet my unfailing love for you will not be shaken nor my covenant of peace be removed," says the Lord, who has compassion on you.

Psalm 36:5 Your love, Lord, reaches to the heavens, your faithfulness to the skies.

1 Kings 8:56-58 [56] "Praise be to the Lord, who has given rest to his people Israel just as he promised. Not one word has failed of all the good promises he gave through his servant Moses. [57] May the Lord our God be with us as he was with our ancestors; may he never leave us nor forsake us. [58] May he turn our hearts to him, to walk in obedience to him and keep the

1 Corinthians 1:9 [9] God is faithful, who has called you into fellowship with his Son, Jesus Christ our Lord.

1 Thessalonians 5:23-24 [23] May God himself, the God of peace, sanctify you through and through. May your whole spirit, soul and body be kept blameless at the coming of our Lord Jesus Christ. [24] The one who calls you is faithful, and he will do it.

Genesis 28:15 [15] I am with you and will watch over you wherever you go, and I will bring you back to this land. I will not leave you until I have done what I have promised you."

1 Corinthians 10:13 [13] No temptation[a] has overtaken you except what is common to mankind. And God is faithful; he will not let you be tempted[b] beyond what you can bear. But when you are tempted,[c] he will also provide a way out so that you can endure it.

2 Timothy 2:13, 19 If we are faithless, he remains faithful, for he cannot disown himself. [19] Nevertheless, God's solid foundation stands firm, sealed with this inscription: "The Lord knows those who are his," and, "Everyone who confesses the name of the Lord must turn away from wickedness."

Joshua 23:14 [14] "Now I am about to go the way of all the earth. You know with all your heart and soul that not one of all the good promises the Lord your God gave you has failed. Every promise has been fulfilled; not one has failed.

1 Kings 8:56-58 [56] "Praise be to the Lord, who has given rest to his people Israel just as he promised. Not one word has failed of all the good promises he gave through his servant Moses. [57] May the Lord our God be with us as he was with our ancestors; may he never leave us nor forsake us. [58] May he turn our hearts to him, to walk in obedience to him and keep the commands, decrees and laws he gave our ancestors.

Deuteronomy 7:8-9 [8] But it was because the Lord loved you and kept the oath, he swore to your ancestors that he brought you out with a mighty hand and redeemed you from the land of slavery, from the power of Pharaoh king of Egypt. [9] Know therefore that the Lord your God is God; he is the faithful God, keeping his covenant of love to a thousand generations of those who love him and keep his commandments.

2 Peter 3:9 [9] The Lord is not slow in keeping his promise, as some understand slowness. Instead, he is patient with you, not wanting anyone to perish, but everyone to come to repentance.

HIS CHURCH

Ephesians 1:19-23 That power is the same as the mighty strength [20] he exerted when he raised Christ from the dead and seated him at his right hand in the heavenly realms, [21] far above all rule and authority, power and dominion, and every name that is invoked, not only in the present age but also in the one to come. [22] And God placed all things under his feet and appointed him to be head over everything for the church, [23] which is his body, the fullness of him who fills everything in every way.

Colossians 1:13, 18 [13] For he has rescued us from the dominion of darkness and brought us into the kingdom of the Son he loves, [14] in whom we have redemption, the forgiveness of sins. [18] And he is the head of the body, the church.

Matthew 16:15-18 [15] "But what about you?" he asked. "Who do you say I am?"

[16] Simon Peter answered, "You are the Messiah, the Son of the living God."

[17] Jesus replied, "Blessed are you, Simon son of Jonah, for this was not revealed to you by flesh and blood, but by my Father in heaven. [18] And I tell you that you are Peter,[a] and on this rock I will build my church, and the gates of Hades[b] will not overcome it.

Ephesians 2:19-22 [19] Consequently, you are no longer foreigners and strangers, but fellow citizens with God's people and also members of his household, [20] built on the foundation of the apostles and prophets, with Christ Jesus himself as the chief cornerstone. [21] In him the whole building is joined together and rises to become a holy temple in the Lord. [22] And in him you too are being built together to become a dwelling in which God lives by his Spirit.

Ephesians 5:29-30 [29] After all, no one ever hated their own body, but they feed and care for them.

Romans 12:4-8 [4] For just as each of us has one body with many members, and these members do not all have the same function, [5] so in Christ we, though many, form one body, and each member belongs to all the others. [6] We have different gifts, according to the grace given to each of us. If your gift is prophesying, then prophesy in accordance with your[a] faith; [7] if it is serving, then serve; if it is teaching, then teach; [8] if it is to encourage, then give encouragement; if it is giving, then give generously; if it is to lead,[b] do it diligently; if it is to show mercy, do it cheerfully.

1 Corinthians 12:12-28 [12] Just as a body, though one, has many parts, but all its many parts form one body, so it is with Christ. [13] For we were all baptized by[a] one Spirit so as to form one body—whether Jews or Gentiles, slave or free—and we were all given the one Spirit to drink. [14] Even so the body is not made up of one part but of many.

[15] Now if the foot should say, "Because I am not a hand, I do not belong to the body," it would not for that reason stop being part of the body. [16] And if the ear should say, "Because I am not an eye, I do not belong to the body," it would not for that reason stop being part of the body. [17] If the whole body were an eye, where would the sense of hearing be? If the whole body were an ear, where would the sense of smell be? [18] But in fact God has placed the parts in the body, every one of them, just as he wanted them to be. [19] If they were all one part, where would the body be? [20] As it is, there are many parts, but one body.

[21] The eye cannot say to the hand, "I don't need you!" And the head cannot say to the feet, "I don't need you!" [22] On the contrary, those parts of the body that seem to be weaker are indispensable, [23] and the parts that we think are less honorable we treat with special honor. And the parts that are unpresentable are treated with special modesty, [24] while our presentable parts need no special treatment. But God has put the body together, giving greater honor to the parts that lacked it, [25] so that there should be no division in the body, but that its parts should have equal concern for each other. [26] If one part suffers, every part suffers with it; if one part is honored, every part

rejoices with it.

[27] Now you are the body of Christ, and each one of you is a part of it. [28] And God has placed in the church first of all apostles, second prophets, third teachers, then miracles, then gifts of healing, of helping, of guidance, and of different kinds of tongues.

1 Thessalonians 5:12-13 [12] Now we ask you, brothers and sisters, to acknowledge those who work hard among you, who care for you in the Lord and who admonish you. [13] Hold them in the highest regard in love because of their work. Live in peace with each other.

Ephesians 4:11-13 [11] So Christ himself gave the apostles, the prophets, the evangelists, the pastors and teachers, [12] to equip his people for works of service, so that the body of Christ may be built up [13] until we all reach unity in the faith and in the knowledge of the Son of God and become mature, attaining to the whole measure of the fullness of Christ.

Psalm 133:1 How good and pleasant it is when God's people live together in unity!

DISCIPLESHIP

Matthew 28:18-20 [18] Then Jesus came to them and said, "All authority in heaven and on earth has been given to me. [19] Therefore go and make disciples of all nations, baptizing them in the name of the Father and of the Son and of the Holy Spirit, [20] and teaching them to obey everything I have commanded you. And surely, I am with you always, to the very end of the age."

Philippians 3:8-9 [8] What is more, I consider everything a loss because of the surpassing worth of knowing Christ Jesus my Lord, for whose sake I have lost all things. I consider them garbage, that I may gain Christ [9] and be found in him, not having a righteousness of my own that comes from the law, but that which is through faith in[a] Christ—the righteousness that comes from God on the basis of faith.

Philippians 4:13 [13] I can do all this through him who gives me strength.

John 12:26 [26] Whoever serves me must follow me; and where I am, my servant also will be. My Father will honor the one who serves me.

Luke 5:27-28 [27] After this, Jesus went out and saw a tax collector by the name of Levi sitting at his tax booth. "Follow me," Jesus said to him, [28] and Levi got up, left everything and followed him.

Luke 9:23-26 23 Then he said to them all: "Whoever wants to be my disciple must deny themselves and take up their cross daily and follow me. 24 For whoever wants to save their life will lose it, but whoever loses their life for me will save it. 25 What good is it for someone to gain the whole world, and yet lose or forfeit their very self? 26 Whoever is ashamed of me and my words, the Son of Man will be ashamed of them when he comes in his glory and in the glory of the Father and of the holy angels.

Hebrews 10:24-25 24 And let us consider how we may spur one another on toward love and good deeds, 25 not giving up meeting together, as some are in the habit of doing, but encouraging one another—and all the more as you see the Day approaching.

Luke 6:40 40 The student is not above the teacher, but everyone who is fully trained will be like their teacher.

Acts 11:25-26 25 Then Barnabas went to Tarsus to look for Saul, 26 and when he found him, he brought him to Antioch. So, for a whole year Barnabas and Saul met with the church and taught great numbers of people. The disciples were called Christians first at Antioch.

STEWARDSHIP

Malachi 3:8-12 ⁸ "Will a mere mortal rob God? Yet you rob me.

"But you ask, 'How are we robbing you?'

"In tithes and offerings. ⁹ You are under a curse—your whole nation—because you are robbing me. ¹⁰ Bring the whole tithe into the storehouse, that there may be food in my house. Test me in this," says the Lord Almighty, "and see if I will not throw open the floodgates of heaven and pour out so much blessing that there will not be room enough to store it. ¹¹ I will prevent pests from devouring your crops, and the vines in your fields will not drop their fruit before it is ripe," says the Lord Almighty. ¹² "Then all the nations will call you blessed, for yours will be a delightful land," says the Lord Almighty.

Mark 10:29-30 ²⁹ "Truly I tell you," Jesus replied, "no one who has left home or brothers or sisters or mother or father or children or fields for me and the gospel ³⁰ will fail to receive a hundred times as much in this present age: homes, brothers, sisters, mothers, children and fields—along with persecutions—and in the age to come eternal life.

1 Corinthians 16:1-2 Now about the collection for the Lord's people: Do what I told the Galatian churches to do. ² On the first day of every week, each one of you should set aside a sum of money in keeping with your income, saving it up, so that when I come no collections will have to be made.

2 **Corinthians 9:6-8** ⁶ Remember this: Whoever sows sparingly will also reap sparingly, and whoever sows generously will also reap generously. ⁷ Each of you should give what you have decided in your heart to give, not reluctantly or under compulsion, for God loves a cheerful giver. ⁸ And God is able to bless you abundantly, so that in all things at all times, having all that you need, you will abound in every good work.

Colossians 3:23-24 ²³ Whatever you do, work at it with all your heart, as working for the Lord, not for human masters, ²⁴ since you know that you will receive an inheritance from the Lord as a reward. It is the Lord Christ you are serving.

Deuteronomy 28:2-3, 5-8, 12-13 [2] All these blessings will come on you and accompany you if you obey the Lord your God: [3] You will be blessed in the city and blessed in the country. [5] Your basket and your kneading trough will be blessed. [6] You will be blessed when you come in and blessed when you go out. [7] The Lord will grant that the enemies who rise up against you will be defeated before you. They will come at you from one direction but flee from you in seven. [12] The Lord will open the heavens, the storehouse of his bounty, to send rain on your land in season and to bless all the work of your hands. You will lend to many nations but will borrow from none. [13] The Lord will make you the head, not the tail. If you pay attention to the commands of the Lord your God that I give you this day and carefully follow them, you will always be at the top, never at the bottom.

[8] The Lord will send a blessing on your barns and on everything you put your hand to. The Lord your God will bless you in the land he is giving you.

Matthew 6:33 [33] But seek first his kingdom and his righteousness, and all these things will be given to you as well.

1 Corinthians 9:17-19 [17] If I preach voluntarily, I have a reward; if not voluntarily, I am simply discharging the trust committed to me. [18] What then is my reward? Just this: that in preaching the gospel I may offer it free of charge, and so not make full use of my rights as a preacher of the gospel. [19] Though I am free and belong to no one, I have made myself a slave to everyone, to win as many as possible.

1 Peter 4:10-11 [10] Each of you should use whatever gift you have received to serve others, as faithful stewards of God's grace in its various forms. [11] If anyone speaks, they should do so as one who speaks the very words of God. If anyone serves, they should do so with the strength God provides, so that in all things God may be praised through Jesus Christ. To him be the glory and the power for ever and ever. Amen.

Hebrews 4:13 ¹³ Nothing in all creation is hidden from God's sight. Everything is uncovered and laid bare before the eyes of him to whom we must give account.

Matthew 6:19-21 [19] "Do not store up for yourselves treasures on earth, where moths and vermin destroy, and where thieves break in and steal. [20] But store up for yourselves treasures in heaven, where moths and vermin do not destroy, and where thieves do not break in and steal. [21] For where your treasure is, there your heart will be also.

2 Corinthians 5:9-10 [9] So we make it our goal to please him, whether we are at home in the body or away from it. [10] For we must all appear before the judgment seat of Christ, so that each of us may receive what is due us for the things done while in the body, whether good or bad.

Proverbs 11:24-25 One person gives freely, yet gains even more; another withholds unduly, but comes to poverty. [25] A generous person will prosper; whoever refreshes others will be refreshed.

Joshua 1:8 [8] Keep this Book of the Law always on your lips; meditate on it day and night, so that you may be careful to do everything written in it. Then you will be prosperous and successful.

Galatians 6:10 [10] Therefore, as we have opportunity, let us do good to all people, especially to those who belong to the family of believers.

Luke 16:10-13 [10] "Whoever can be trusted with very little can also be trusted with much, and whoever is dishonest with very little will also be dishonest with much. [11] So if you have not been trustworthy in handling worldly wealth, who will trust you with true riches? [12] And if you have not been trustworthy with someone else's property, who will give you property of your own? [13] "No one can serve two masters. Either you will hate the one and love the other, or you will be devoted to the one and despise the other. You cannot serve both God and money."

FORGIVING OTHERS

Matthew 6:14-15 [14] For if you forgive other people when they sin against you, your heavenly Father will also forgive you. [15] But if you do not forgive others their sins, your Father will not forgive your sins.

Matthew 18:21-22 [21] Then Peter came up and said to Him, "Lord, how many times shall my brother sin against me and I *still* forgive him? Up to seven times?" [22] Jesus *said to him, "I do not say to you, up to seven times, but up to seventy-seven times.

Luke 17:3-4 [3] Be on your guard! If your brother sins, rebuke him; and if he repents, forgive him. [4] And if he sins against you seven times a day, and returns to you seven times, saying, 'I repent,' you shall forgive him."

Colossians 3:12-13 [12] So, as those who have been chosen of God, holy and beloved, put on a heart of compassion, kindness, humility, gentleness, *and* [a]patience; [13] bearing with one another, and forgiving each other, whoever has a complaint against anyone; just as the Lord forgave you, so *must* you *do* also.

Matthew 5:44 [44] But I say to you, love your enemies and pray for those who persecute you,

1 Peter 3:9-10 [9] Do not do wrong to repay a wrong, and do not insult to repay an insult. But repay with a blessing, because you yourselves were called to do this so that you might receive a blessing. [10] The Scripture says, "A person must do these things: to enjoy life and have many happy days. He must not say evil things, and he must not tell lies.

Ephesians 4:31-32 [31] Do not be bitter or angry or mad. Never shout angrily or say things to hurt others. Never do anything evil. [32] Be kind and loving to each other and forgive each other just as God forgave you in Christ.

Philippians 3:13-14 [13] Brothers and sisters, I know that I have not yet reached that goal, but there is one thing I always do. Forgetting the past and straining toward what is ahead, [14] I keep trying to reach the goal and get the prize for which God called me through Christ to the life above.

Isaiah 43:18, 25 The Lord says, "Forget what happened before, and do not think about the past.   "I, I am the One who erases all your sins, for my sake; I will not remember your sins.

Mark 11:25 And whenever you stand praying, forgive, if you have anything against anyone, so that your Father also who is in heaven may forgive you your trespasses."

Luke 6:37 "Judge not, and you will not be judged; condemn not, and you will not be condemned; forgive, and you will be forgiven.

Matthew 5:23-24 So if you are offering your gift at the altar and there remember that your brother has something against you, leave your gift there before the altar and go. First be reconciled to your brother, and then come and offer your gift.

THE
QUALITIES OF A CHRISTIAN

Luke 10:27 "You shall love the Lord your God with all your heart and with all your soul and with all your strength and with all your mind, and your neighbor as yourself."

Galatians 6:9-10 [9] Let us not become weary in doing good, for at the proper time we will reap a harvest if we do not give up. [10] Therefore, as we have opportunity, let us do good to all people, especially to those who belong to the family of believers.

Luke 6:35 But love your enemies, and do good, and lend, expecting nothing in return, and your reward will be great, and you will be sons of the Most High, for he is kind to the ungrateful and the evil.

Colossians 3:12-17 [12] Therefore, as God's chosen people, holy and dearly loved, clothe yourselves with compassion, kindness, humility, gentleness and patience. [13] Bear with each other and forgive one another if any of you has a grievance against someone. Forgive as the Lord forgave you. [14] And over all these virtues put on love, which binds them all together in perfect unity. [15] Let the peace of Christ rule in your hearts, since as members of one body you were called to peace. And be thankful. [16] Let the message of Christ dwell among you richly as you teach and admonish one another with all wisdom through psalms, hymns, and songs from the Spirit, singing to God with gratitude in your hearts. [17] And whatever you do, whether in word or deed, do it all in the name of the Lord Jesus, giving thanks to God the Father through him.

Romans 12:2 [2] Do not conform to the pattern of this world, but be transformed by the renewing of your mind. Then you will be able to test and approve what God's will is—his good, pleasing and perfect will.

Galatians 5:22-23 [22] But the fruit of the Spirit is love, joy, peace, forbearance, kindness, goodness, faithfulness, [23] gentleness and self-control. Against such things there is no law.

Philippians 4:8 - Finally, brethren, whatsoever things are true, whatsoever things are honest, whatsoever things are just, whatsoever things are pure, whatsoever things are lovely, whatsoever things are of good report; if there be any virtue, and if there be any praise, think

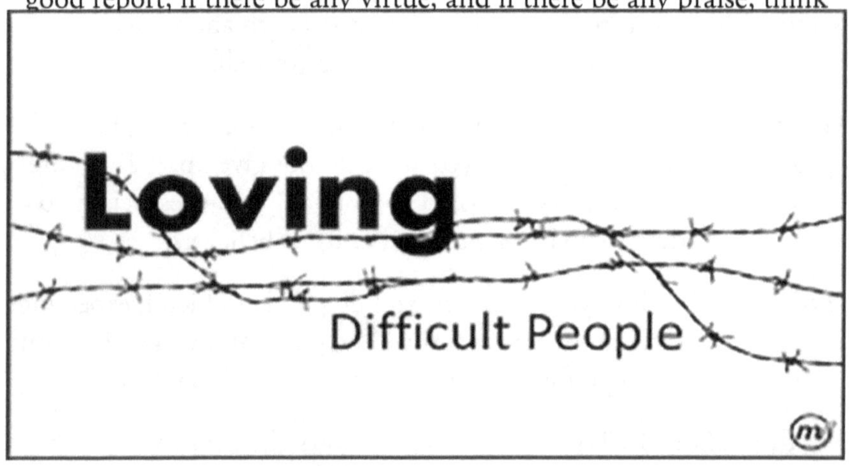

on these things.

2 Peter 1:5-7 - For this very reason, make every effort to supplement your faith with virtue, and virtue with knowledge, and knowledge with self-control, and self-control with steadfastness, and steadfastness with godliness, and godliness with brotherly affection, and brotherly affection with love.

Romans 13:14 - Let the Lord Jesus Christ be as near to you as the clothes you wear. Then you won't try to satisfy your selfish desires.

Psalm 15:1-5 ^{1} Lord, who may dwell in your sacred tent? Who may live on your holy mountain? ^{2} The one whose walk is blameless, who does what is righteous, who speaks the truth from their heart; ^{3} whose tongue utters no slander, who does no wrong to a neighbor, and casts no slur on others; ^{4} who despises a vile person but honors those who fear the Lord; who keeps an oath even when it hurts, and does not change their mind; ^{5} who lends money to the poor without interest; who does not accept a bribe against the innocent. Whoever does these things will never be shaken.

LOVING PEOPLE YOU
FIND DIFFICULT

Luke 6:27-36 "But I say to you who hear, Love your enemies, do good to those who hate you, bless those who curse you, pray for those who abuse you. To one who strikes you on the cheek, offer the other also, and from one who takes away your cloak do not withhold your tunic either. Give to everyone who begs from you, and from one who takes away your goods do not demand them back. And as you wish that others would do to you, do so to them.

2 Timothy 2:23-26 Have nothing to do with foolish, ignorant controversies; you know that they breed quarrels. And the Lord's servant must not be quarrelsome but kind to everyone, able to teach, patiently enduring evil, correcting his opponents with gentleness. God may perhaps grant them repentance leading to a knowledge of the truth, and they may come to their senses and escape from the snare of the devil, after being captured by him to do his will.

Romans 12:9-21 Let love be genuine. Abhor what is evil; hold fast to what is good. Love one another with brotherly affection. Outdo one another in showing honor. Do not be slothful in zeal, be fervent in spirit, serve the Lord. Rejoice in hope, be patient in tribulation, be constant in prayer. Contribute to the needs of the saints and seek to show hospitality.

1 Corinthians 13:4-7 Love is patient and kind; love does not envy or boast; it is not arrogant or rude. It does not insist on its own way; it is not irritable or resentful; it does not rejoice at wrongdoing but rejoices with the truth. Love bears all things, believes all things, hopes all things, endures all things.

Proverbs 15:1-2 A soft answer turns away wrath, but a harsh word stirs up anger. The tongue of the wise commends knowledge, but the mouths of fools pour out folly.

Matthew 5:46 For if you love those who love you, what reward do you have? Do not even the tax collectors do the same?

John 15:12 "This is my commandment, that you love one another as I have loved you.

Matthew 18:15 "If your brother sins against you, go and tell him his fault, between you and him alone. If he listens to you, you have gained your brother.

Matthew 5:38-48 [38] "You have heard that it was said, 'Eye for eye, and tooth for tooth.'[a] [39] But I tell you, do not resist an evil person. If anyone slaps you on the right cheek, turn to them the other cheek also. [40] And if anyone wants to sue you and take your shirt, hand over your coat as well. [41] If anyone forces you to go one mile, go with them two miles. [42] Give to the one who asks you, and do not turn away from the one who wants to borrow from you. [43] "You have heard that it was said, 'Love your neighbor[b] and hate your enemy.' [44] But I tell you, love your enemies and pray for those who persecute you, [45] that you may be children of your Father in heaven. He causes his sun to rise on the evil and the good, and sends rain on the righteous and the unrighteous. [46] If you love those who love you, what reward will you get? Are not even the tax collectors doing that? [47] And if you greet only your own people, what are you doing more than others? Do not even pagans do that? [48] Be perfect, therefore, as your heavenly Father is perfect.

Luke 6:32 "If you love those who love you, what benefit is that to you? For even sinners love those who love them.

Proverbs 9:7-9 Whoever corrects a scoffer gets himself abuse, and he who reproves a wicked man incurs injury. Do not reprove a scoffer, or he will hate you; reprove a wise man, and he will love you. Give instruction to a wise man, and he will be still wiser; teach a righteous man, and he will increase in learning.

Proverbs 10:12 Hatred stirs up strife, but love covers all offenses.

John 13:35 By this all people will know that you are my disciples, if you have love for one another."

John 3:16 "For God so loved the world, that he gave his only Son, that whoever believes in him should not perish but have eternal life.

Romans 5:8 But God shows his love for us in that while we were still sinners, Christ died for us.

1 Peter 4:8 Above all, keep loving one another earnestly, since love covers a multitude of sins.

Mark 12:30 And you shall love the Lord your God with all your heart and with all your soul and with all your mind and with all your strength.'

Romans 12:18 If possible, so far as it depends on you, live peaceably with all.

Proverbs 17:17 A friend loves at all times, and a brother is born for adversity.

John 3:16-17 "For God so loved the world, that he gave his only Son, that whoever believes in him should not perish but have eternal life. For God did not send his Son into the world to condemn the world, but in order that the world might be saved through him.

John 15:13 Greater love has no one than this, that someone lay down his life for his friends.

Philippians 2:3 Do nothing from rivalry or conceit, but in humility count others more significant than yourselves.

Philippians 4:13 I can do all things through him who strengthens me.

1 John 4:19 We love because he first loved us.

Ephesians 4:2 With all humility and gentleness, with patience, bearing with one another in love,

1 Corinthians 13:13 So now faith, hope, and love abide, these three; but the greatest of these is love.

Luke 6:35 But love your enemies, and do good, and lend, expecting nothing in return, and your reward will be great, and you will be sons of the Most High, for he is kind to the ungrateful and the evil.

1 Corinthians 13:4-8 Love is patient and kind; love does not envy or boast; it is not arrogant or rude. It does not insist on its own way; it is not irritable or resentful; it does not rejoice at wrongdoing but rejoices with the truth. Love bears all things, believes all things, hopes all things, endures all things. Love never ends. As for prophecies, they will pass away; as for tongues, they will cease; as for knowledge, it will pass away.

Colossians 3:14 And above all these put on love, which binds everything together in perfect harmony.

1 John 4:7-8 Beloved, let us love one another, for love is from God, and whoever loves has been born of God and knows God. Anyone who does not love does not know God, because God is love.

Luke 6:27 "But I say to you who hear, Love your enemies, do good to those who hate you,

Proverbs 12:16 The vexation (aggravation, agitation, annoy) of a fool is known at once, but the prudent (careful, cautious, discreet) ignores an insult.

1 Corinthians 13:1-13 If I speak in the tongues of men and of angels, but have not love, I am a noisy gong or a clanging cymbal. And if I have prophetic powers, and understand all mysteries and all knowledge, and if I have all faith, so as to remove mountains, but have not love, I am nothing. If I give away all I have, and if I deliver up my body to be burned, but have not love, I gain nothing. Love is patient and kind; love does not envy or boast; it is not arrogant or rude. It does not insist on its own way; it is not irritable or resentful;

...

1 Corinthians 16:14 Let all that you do be done in love.

Romans 12:10 Love one another with brotherly affection. Outdo one another in showing honor.

Leviticus 19:18 You shall not take vengeance or bear a grudge against the sons of your own people, but you shall love your neighbor as yourself: I am the Lord.

1 John 3:1 See what kind of love the Father has given to us, that we should be called children of God; and so we are. The reason why the world does not know us is that it did not know him.

Ephesians 4:2-3 With all humility and gentleness, with patience, bearing with one another in love, eager to maintain the unity of the Spirit in the bond of peace.

Romans 13:8 Owe no one anything, except to love each other, for the one who loves another has fulfilled the law.

Romans 8:28 And we know that for those who love God all things work together for good, for those who are called according to his purpose.

Ecclesiastes 4:9-12 Two are better than one, because they have a good reward for their toil. For if they fall, one will lift up his fellow. But woe to him who is alone when he falls and has not another to lift him up! Again, if two lie together, they keep warm, but how can one keep warm alone? And though a man might prevail against one who is alone, two will withstand him—a threefold cord is not quickly broken.

1 Chronicles 16:11 Seek the Lord and his strength; seek his presence continually!

1 Peter 5:6-7 Humble yourselves, therefore, under the mighty hand of God so that at the proper time he may exalt you, casting all your anxieties on him, because he cares for you.

Galatians 5:13 For you were called to freedom, brothers. Only do not use your freedom as an opportunity for the flesh, but through love serve one another.

Matthew 7:7 "Ask, and it will be given to you; seek, and you will find; knock, and it will be opened to you.

Matthew 5:44-45 But I say to you, Love your enemies and pray for those who persecute you, so that you may be sons of your Father who is in heaven. For he makes his sun rise on the evil and on the good, and sends rain on the just and on the unjust.

Proverbs 28:13 Whoever conceals his transgressions will not prosper, but he who confesses and forsakes them will obtain mercy.

1 John 4:7 Beloved, let us love one another, for love is from God, and whoever loves has been born of God and knows God.

John 13:34-35 A new commandment I give to you, that you love one another: just as I have loved you, you also are to love one another. By this all people will know that you are my disciples, if you have love for one another."

Matthew 7:1-29 "Judge not, that you be not judged. For with the judgment, you pronounce you will be judged, and with the measure you use it will be measured to you. Why do you see the speck that is in your brother's eye, but do not notice the log that is in your own eye? Or how can you say to your brother, 'Let me take the speck out of your eye,' when there is the log in your own eye? You hypocrite, first take the log out of your own eye, and then you will see clearly to take the speck out of your brother's eye. ...

1 Peter 1:22 Having purified your souls by your obedience to the truth for a sincere brotherly love, love one another earnestly from a pure heart,

Romans 12:20 To the contrary, "if your enemy is hungry, feed him; if he is thirsty, give him something to drink; for by so doing you will hear burning coals on his head."

1 John 4:16 So we have come to know and to believe the love that God has for us. God is love, and whoever abides in love abides in God, and God abides in him.

Proverbs 17:27-28 Whoever restrains his words has knowledge, and he who has a cool spirit is a man of understanding. Even a fool who keeps silent is considered wise; when he closes his lips, he is deemed intelligent.

Galatians 5:22 But the fruit of the Spirit is love, joy, peace, patience, kindness, goodness, faithfulness,

Romans 3:23 For all have sinned and fall short of the glory of God.

Deuteronomy 31:6 Be strong and courageous. Do not fear or be in dread of them, for it is the Lord your God who goes with you. He will not leave you or forsake you."

Exodus 20:12 "Honor your father and your mother, that your days may be long in the land that the Lord your God is giving you.

1 Peter 5:10 And after you have suffered a little while, the God of all grace, who has called you to his eternal glory in Christ, will himself restore, confirm, strengthen, and establish you.

1 Peter 3:9 Do not repay evil for evil or reviling for reviling, but on the contrary, bless, for to this you were called, that you may obtain a blessing.

Philippians 2:3-4 Do nothing from rivalry or conceit, but in humility count others more significant than yourselves. Let each of you look not only to his own interests, but also to the interests of others.

Ephesians 4:15 Rather, speaking the truth in love, we are to grow up in every way into him who is the head, into Christ,

Romans 8:37-39 No, in all these things we are more than conquerors through him who loved us. For I am sure that neither death nor life, nor angels nor rulers, nor things present nor things to come, nor powers, nor height nor depth, nor anything else in all creation, will be able to separate us from the love of God in Christ Jesus our Lord.

John 14:27 Peace I leave with you; my peace I give to you. Not as the world gives do I give to you. Let not your hearts be troubled, neither let them be afraid.

Isaiah 41:10 Fear not, for I am with you; be not dismayed, for I am your God; I will strengthen you, I will help you, I will uphold you with my righteous right hand.

Matthew 5:9 "Blessed are the peacemakers, for they shall be called sons of God.

Psalm 91:1-16 He who dwells in the shelter of the Most High will abide in the shadow of the Almighty. I will say to the Lord, "My refuge and my fortress, my God, in whom I trust." For he will deliver you from the snare of the fowler and from the deadly pestilence. He will cover you with his pinions, and under his wings you will find refuge; his faithfulness is a shield and buckler. You will not fear the terror of the night, nor the arrow that flies by day.

1 Thessalonians 5:15 See that no one repays anyone evil for evil, but always seek to do good to one another and to everyone.

1 John 4:11 Beloved, if God so loved us, we also ought to love one another.

Ephesians 4:32 Be kind to one another, tenderhearted, forgiving one another, as God in Christ forgave you.

Mark 11:25 And whenever you stand praying, forgive, if you have anything against anyone, so that your Father also who is in heaven may forgive you your trespasses."

1 John 3:18 Little children, let us not love in word or talk but indeed and in truth.

2 Timothy 2:24-26 And the Lord's servant must not be quarrelsome but kind to everyone, able to teach, patiently enduring evil, correcting his opponents with gentleness. God may perhaps grant them repentance leading to a knowledge of the truth, and they may come to their senses and escape from the snare of the devil, after being captured by him to do his will.

Romans 12:3 For by the grace given to me I say to everyone among you not to think of himself more highly than he ought to think, but to think with sober judgment, each according to the measure of faith that God has assigned.

Ephesians 5:2 And walk in love, as Christ loved us and gave himself up for us, a fragrant offering and sacrifice to God.

Galatians 2:20 I have been crucified with Christ. It is no longer I who live, but Christ who lives in me. And the life I now live in the flesh I live by faith in the Son of God, who loved me and gave himself for me.

Matthew 7:1 "Judge not, that you be not judged.

Matthew 6:24 "No one can serve two masters, for either he will hate the one and love the other, or he will be devoted to the one and despise the other. You cannot serve God and money.

Proverbs 3:3-4 Let not steadfast love and faithfulness forsake you; bind them around your neck; write them on the tablet of your heart. So, you will find favor and good success in the sight of God and man.

Philippians 2:13-15 [13] For God is the one who, for his good purpose, works in you both to desire and to work. [14] Do everything without grumbling or questioning, [15] that you may be blameless and innocent, children of God without blemish in the midst of a crooked and perverse generation,[a] among whom you shine like lights in the world.

Galatians 5:14 For the whole law is fulfilled in one word: "You shall love your neighbor as yourself."

Isaiah 40:29 He gives power to the faint, and to him who has no might he increases strength.

Romans 13:10 Love does no wrong to a neighbor; therefore, love is the fulfilling of the law.

Romans 5:5 And hope does not put us to shame, because God's love has been poured into our hearts through the Holy Spirit who has been given to us.

Matthew 7:12 "So whatever you wish that others would do to you, do also to them, for this is the Law and the Prophets.

1 John 4:12 No one has ever seen God; if we love one another, God abides in us, and his love is perfected in us.

CHRISTIAN
HARMONY AND FELLOWSHIP

Hebrews 10:22-25 ²² let us come near to God with a sincere heart and a sure faith, because we have been made free from a guilty conscience, and our bodies have been washed with pure water. ²³ Let us hold firmly to the hope that we have confessed, because we can trust God to do what he promised. ²⁴ Let us think about each other and help each other to show love and do good deeds. ²⁵ You should not stay away from the church meetings, as some are doing, but you should meet together and encourage each other. Do this even more as you see the day coming.

Romans 12:10 ¹⁰ Love each other like brothers and sisters. Give each other more honor than you want for yourselves.

1 Peter 4:9 ⁹ Open your homes to each other, without complaining.

Ephesians 5:2, 19-22 ² Live a life of love just as Christ loved us and gave himself for us as a sweet-smelling offering and sacrifice to God. ¹⁹ Speak to each other with psalms, hymns, and spiritual songs, singing and making music in your hearts to the Lord. ²⁰ Always give thanks to God the Father for everything, in the name of our Lord Jesus Christ.

1 John 1:3, 7 ³ We announce to you what we have seen and heard, because we want you also to have fellowship with us. Our fellowship is with God the Father and with his Son, Jesus Christ. ⁷ But if we live in the light, as God is in the light, we can share fellowship with each other. Then the blood of Jesus, God's Son, cleanses us from every sin.

Colossians 3:16-17 ¹⁶ Let the teaching of Christ live in you richly. Use all wisdom to teach and instruct each other by singing psalms, hymns, and spiritual songs with thankfulness in your hearts to God. ¹⁷ Everything you do or say should be done to obey Jesus your Lord. And in all you do, give thanks to God the Father through Jesus.

Philippians 2:1-2 Does your life in Christ give you strength? Does his love comfort you? Do we share together in the spirit? Do you have mercy and kindness? ² If so, make me very happy by having the same thoughts, sharing the same love, and having one mind and purpose.

John 17:11, 21-23 ¹¹ I am coming to you; I will not stay in the world any longer. But they are still in the world. Holy Father, keep them safe by the ²¹ Father, I pray that they can be one. As you are in me and I am in you, I pray that they can also be one in us. Then the world will believe that you sent me. ²² I have given these people the glory that you gave me so that they can be one, just as you and I are one. ²³ I will be in them, and you will be in me so that they will be completely one. Then the world will know that you sent me and that you loved them just as much as you loved me. power of your name, the name you gave me, so that they will be one, just as you and I are one.

Acts 2:1, 42, 46-47 When the day of Pentecost came, they were all together in one place. … ⁴² They spent their time learning the apostles' teaching, sharing, breaking bread,[a] and praying together. … ⁴⁶ The believers met together in the Temple every day. They ate together in their homes, happy to share their food with joyful hearts. ⁴⁷ They praised God and were liked by all the people. Every day the Lord added those who were being saved to the group of believers.

Romans 15:5-7 ⁵ May the patience and encouragement that come from God allow you to live in harmony with each other the way Christ Jesus wants. ⁶ Then you will all be joined together, and you will give glory to God the Father of our Lord Jesus Christ. ⁷ Christ accepted you, so you should accept each other, which will bring glory to God.

Psalm 133:1 It is good and pleasant when God's people live together in peace!

1 Peter 3:15 ¹⁵ But respect Christ as the holy Lord in your hearts. Always be ready to answer everyone who asks you to explain about the hope you have,

Galatians 6:2, 10 [2] By helping each other with your troubles, you truly obey the law of Christ. [10] If we have the opportunity to help anyone, we should do it. But we should give special attention to those who are in the family of believers.

THE CHRISTIAN'S RESPONSIBILITY

1 Timothy 5:8 [8] Whoever does not care for his own relatives, especially his own family members, has turned against the faith and is worse than someone who does not believe in God.

Mark 16:15 [15] Jesus said to his followers, "Go everywhere in the world, and tell the Good News to everyone.

Acts 1:8 [8] But when the Holy Spirit comes to you, you will receive power. You will be my witnesses—in Jerusalem, in all of Judea, in Samaria, and in every part of the world."

Matthew 25:35-40 [35] I was hungry, and you gave me food. I was thirsty, and you gave me something to drink. I was alone and away from home, and you invited me into your house. [36] I was without clothes, and you gave me something to wear. I was sick, and you cared for me. I was in prison, and you visited me.' [37] "Then the good people will answer, 'Lord, when did we see you hungry and give you food, or thirsty and give you something to drink? [38] When did we see you alone and away from home and invite you into our house? When did we see you without clothes and give you something to wear? [39] When did we see you sick or in prison and care for you?' [40] "Then the King will answer, 'I tell you the truth, anything you did for even the least of my people here, you also did for me.'

Matthew 10:42 [42] Those who give one of these little ones a cup of cold water because they are my followers will truly get their reward."

Romans 12:6-8 [6] We all have different gifts, each of which came because of the grace God gave us. The person who has the gift of prophecy should use that gift in agreement with the faith. [7] Anyone who has the gift of serving should serve. Anyone who has the gift of teaching should teach. [8] Whoever has the gift of encouraging others should encourage. Whoever has the gift of giving to others should give freely. Anyone who has the gift of being a leader should try hard when he leads. Whoever has the gift of showing mercy to others should do so with joy.

Luke 12:47-48 ⁴⁷ "The servant who knows what his master wants but is not ready, or who does not do what the master wants, will be beaten with many blows! ⁴⁸ But the servant who does not know what his master wants and does things that should be punished will be beaten with few blows. From everyone who has been given much, much will be demanded. And from the one trusted with much, much more will be expected.

Luke 16:10 ¹⁰ Whoever can be trusted with a little can also be trusted with a lot, and whoever is dishonest with a little is dishonest with a lot.

Matthew 5:13-16 ¹³ "You are the salt of the earth. But if the salt loses its salty taste, it cannot be made salty again. It is good for nothing, except to be thrown out and walked on. ¹⁴ "You are the light that gives light to the world. A city that is built on a hill cannot be hidden. ¹⁵ And people don't hide a light under a bowl. They put it on a lampstand so the light shines for all the people in the house. ¹⁶ In the same way, you should be a light for other people. Live so that they will see the good things you do and will praise your Father in heaven.

Colossians 3:23 ²³ In all the work you are doing, work the best you can. Work as if you were doing it for the Lord, not for people.

Ephesians 6:4 ⁴ Fathers, do not make your children angry, but raise them with the training and teaching of the Lord.

Hebrews 6:10-12 ¹⁰ God is fair; he will not forget the work you did and the love you showed for him by helping his people. And he will remember that you are still helping them. ¹¹ We want each of you to go on with the same hard work all your lives so you will surely get what you hope for. ¹² We do not want you to become lazy. Be like those who through faith and patience will receive what God has promised.

James 2:15-17 ¹⁵ A brother or sister in Christ might need clothes or food. ¹⁶ If you say to that person, "God be with you! I hope you stay warm and get plenty to eat," but you do not give what that person needs, your words are worth nothing. ¹⁷ In the same way, faith by itself—that does nothing—is dead.

Luke 3:10-11 [10] The people asked John, "Then what should we do?" [11] John answered, "If you have two shirts, share with the person who does not have one. If you have food, share that also." [12] Even tax collectors came to John to be baptized. They said to him, "Teacher, what should we do?"

Romans 12:3 [3] Because God has given me a special gift, I have something to say to everyone among you. Do not think you are better than you are. You must decide what you really are by the amount of faith God has given you.

James 4:17 Anyone who knows the right thing to do, but does not do it, is sinning.

Galatians 6:1-5 Brothers and sisters, if someone in your group does something wrong, you who are spiritual should go to that person and gently help make him right again. But be careful, because you might be tempted to sin, too. [2] By helping each other with your troubles, you truly obey the law of Christ. [3] If anyone thinks he is important when he really is not, he is only fooling himself. [4] Each person should judge his own actions and not compare himself with others. Then he can be proud for what he himself has done. [5] Each person must be responsible for himself.

Deuteronomy 11:1, 18-19 Love the Lord your God and always obey his orders, rules, laws, and commands. [18] Remember my words with your whole being. Write them down and tie them to your hands as a sign; tie them on your foreheads to remind you. [19] Teach them well to your children, talking about them when you sit at home and walk along the road, when you lie down and when you get up.

1 John 3:16-23 [16] "God loved the world so much that he gave his one and only Son so that whoever believes in him may not be lost but have eternal life. [17] God did not send his Son into the world to judge the world guilty, but to save the world through him. [18] People who believe in God's Son are not judged guilty. Those who do not believe have already been judged guilty, because they have not believed in God's one and only Son. [19] They are judged by this fact: The Light has come into the world, but they did not want light. They wanted darkness, because they were doing evil things. [20] All who do evil hate the light and will not come to the light, because it will show all the evil things they do. [21] But those who follow the true way come to the light, and it shows that the things they do were done through God."

Deuteronomy 6:6-9 [6] Always remember these commands I give you today. [7] Teach them to your children and talk about them when you sit at home and walk along the road, when you lie down and when you get up. [8] Write them down and tie them to your hands as a sign. Tie them on your forehead to remind you, [9] and write them on your doors and gates.

Proverbs 22:4 Respecting the Lord and not being proud will bring you wealth, honor, and life.

TRUTH
ABOUT THE WILL OF GOD

Proverbs 8:17 "I love those who love me, and those who diligently seek me will find me.

Deuteronomy 4:29 But from there, you will seek the LORD your God, and you will find Him if you search for Him with all your heart and all your soul.

Proverbs 3:6 Seek His will in all you do, and he will show you which path to take.

Luke 11:9-10 So I say to you, ask, and it will be given to you; seek, and you will find; knock, and it will be opened to you.

Jeremiah 29:13 You will seek Me and find Me when you search for Me with all your heart.

James 1:5-6 If you do not have wisdom, ask God for it. He is always ready to give it to you and will never say you are wrong for asking. [6] You must have faith as you ask Him. You must not doubt. Anyone who doubts is like a wave which is pushed around by the sea.

Proverbs 6:20, 22-23 [20] My son, keep the teaching of your father, and do not turn away from the teaching of your mother. … [22] They will lead you when you walk. They will watch over you when you sleep, and they will talk with you when you wake up. [23] For the word is a lamp. The teaching is a light, and strong words that punish are the way of life.

Joshua 1:8-9 [8] This book of the Law must not leave your mouth. Think about it day and night, so you may be careful to do all that is written in it. Then all will go well with you. You will receive many good things. [9] Have I not told you? Be strong and have strength of heart! Do not be afraid or lose faith. For the Lord your God is with you anywhere you go."

1 Thessalonians 4:3-4 [3] God wants you to be holy. You must keep away from sex sins. [4] God wants each of you to use his body in the right way by keeping it holy and by respecting it.

1 Thessalonians 5:16-18 [16] Be full of joy all the time. [17] Never stop praying. [18] In everything give thanks. This is what God wants you to do because of Christ Jesus.

Amos 5:4-6 For thus says the LORD to the house of Israel, "Seek Me that you may live.

Psalm 69:32 The humble shall see this, and be glad: and your heart shall live that seek God.

Isaiah 40:31 They who wait upon the Lord will get new strength. They will rise up with wings like eagles. They will run and not get tired. They will walk and not become weak.

2 Chronicles 16:9 For the eyes of the LORD range throughout the earth to strengthen those whose hearts are fully committed to him.

1 Chronicles 16:11 Seek the LORD and His strength; Seek His face continually.

Psalm 105:3-4 Glory in his holy name; let the hearts of those who seek the Lord rejoice. Look to the Lord and his strength; seek his face always.

1 Chronicles 16:10 Let the heart of those who seek the Lord be glad.

Psalm 70:4 But may all who seek you rejoice and be glad in you may those who long for your saving help always say, "The Lord is great!"

Psalm 34:4-5 I sought the Lord, and he answered me; he delivered me from all my fears. Those who look to him are radiant; their faces are never covered with shame.

Psalm 145:18-20 The Lord is near to all who call on him, to all who call on him in truth. He fulfills the desires of those who fear him; he hears their cry and saves them.

Psalm 107:13-14 Then they cried to the Lord in their trouble, and he saved them from their distress. He brought them out of darkness, the utter darkness, and broke away their chains.

Proverbs 28:5 Evil men do not understand justice, But those who seek the LORD understand all things.

Isaiah 49:23 Then you will know that I am the Lord; those who hope in me will not be disappointed."

Psalm 34:10 The lions may grow weak and hungry, but those who seek the Lord lack no good thing.

Proverbs 2:3-6 Indeed, if you call out for insight and cry aloud for understanding, and if you look for it as for silver and search for it as for hidden treasure, then you will understand the fear of the Lord and find the knowledge of God. For the Lord gives wisdom; from his mouth come knowledge and understanding.

Lamentation 3:21-25 This I recall to my mind; therefore, I have hope. Through the Lord's mercies, we are not consumed, because His compassions fail not. They are new every morning; great is Your faithfulness. "The Lord is my portion," says my soul, "Therefore I hope in Him!" The Lord is good to those who wait for Him, to the soul who seeks Him.

Hebrews 11:6 And without faith, it is impossible to please Him, for he who comes to God must believe that He is and that He is a rewarder of those who seek Him.

Lamentations 3:25 The LORD is good to them that wait for him, to the soul that seeks him.

Psalm 119:2 How blessed are those who observe His testimonies, who seek Him with all their heart?

Hosea 10:12 Sow with a view to righteousness, Reap in accordance with kindness; Break up your fallow ground, For it is time to seek the LORD Until He comes to rain righteousness on you.

Psalm 24:5-6 They will receive blessing from the Lord and vindication from God their Savior. Such is the generation of those who seek him, who seek your face, God of Jacob.

Psalm 119:10 I seek you with all my heart; do not let me stray from your commands

Psalm 63:1 O God, You are my God; I shall seek You earnestly; My soul thirsts for You, my flesh yearns for You, In a dry and weary land where there is no water.

Psalm 27:4-5 One thing I have asked from the LORD, that I shall seek: That I may dwell in the house of the LORD all the days of my life, To behold the beauty of the LORD And to meditate in His temple. For in the day of trouble He will conceal me in His tabernacle; In the secret place of His tent, He will hide me; He will lift me up on a rock.

ANSWERED PRAYER

Matthew 7:7-8 If you believe, you will get anything you ask for in prayer.

Isaiah 65:24 I will provide for their needs before they ask, and I will help them while they are still asking for help.

Ephesians 6:18 And pray in the Spirit on all occasions with all kinds of prayers and requests. With this in mind, be alert and always keep on praying for all the Lord's people.

Matthew 18:19-20 [19] Again I tell you this: If two of you agree on earth about anything you pray for, it will be done for you by My Father in heaven. [20] For where two or three are gathered together in My name, there I am with them."

John 15:7 If you remain in Me and My Words remain in you, ask whatever you wish, and it will be done for you.

Philippians 4:6 Do not be anxious about anything, but in every situation, by prayer and petition, with thanksgiving, present your requests to God.

John 9:31 We know that God does not hear sinners; but if anyone is God-fearing and does His will, He hears him.

1 Peter 3:12 For the eyes of the Lord are on the righteous and His ears are attentive to their prayer, but the face of the Lord is against those who do evil.

Psalm 40:1 I waited patiently for the Lord; he turned to me and heard my cry.

John 16:23-24 In that day you will no longer ask Me anything. Very truly I tell you, My Father will give you whatever you ask in My Name. Until now you have not asked for anything in My Name. Ask and you will receive, and your joy will be complete.

James 1:6 In that day you will no longer ask Me anything. Very truly I tell you, My Father will give you whatever you ask in My Name. Until now you have not asked for anything in My Name. Ask and you will receive, and your joy will be complete.

Matthew 21:21-22 Jesus replied, "Truly I tell you, if you have faith and do not doubt, not only can you do what was done to the fig tree, but also you can say to this mountain, 'Go, throw yourself into the sea,' and it will be done. If you believe, you will receive whatever you ask for in prayer.'"

2 Chronicles 7:14 If My people, who are called by My Name, will humble themselves and pray and seek my face, and turn from their wicked ways, then I will hear from Heaven, and I will forgive their sin and heal their land.

James 5:15-16 And the prayer offered in faith will make the sick person well; the Lord will raise them up. If they have sinned, they will be forgiven. Therefore, confess your sins to each other and pray for each other so that you may be healed. The prayer of a righteous person is powerful and effective.

James 4:2 You desire but do not have, so you kill. You covet but you cannot get what you want, so you quarrel and fight. You do not have because you do not ask God.

Matthew 7:10 If you, then, though you are evil, know how to give good gifts to your children, how much more will your Father in Heaven give good gifts to those who ask Him?

Mark 11:24-25 [24] Because of this, I say to you, whatever you ask for when you pray, have faith that you will receive it. Then you will get it. [25] When you stand to pray, if you have anything against anyone, forgive him. Then your Father in heaven will forgive your sins also.

MARRIAGE

Ephesians 5:22-33 [22] Wives, subject yourselves to your own husbands, as to the Lord. [23] For the husband is the head of the wife, as Christ also is the head of the church, He Himself being the Savior of the body. [24] But as the church is subject to Christ, so also the wives ought to be to their husbands in everything.

[25] Husbands, love your wives, just as Christ also loved the church and gave Himself up for her, [26] so that He might sanctify her, having cleansed her by the washing of water with the word, [27] that He might present to Himself the church [c]in all her glory, having no spot or wrinkle or any such thing; but that she would be holy and blameless. [28] So husbands also ought to love their own wives as their own bodies. He who loves his own wife loves himself; [29] for no one ever hated his own flesh, but nourishes and cherishes it, just as Christ also does the church, [30] because we are parts of His body. [31] For this reason a man shall leave his father and his mother and be joined to his wife, and the two shall become one flesh. [32] This mystery is great; but I am speaking with reference to Christ and the church. [33] Nevertheless, as for you individually, each husband is to love his own wife the same as himself, and the wife must see to it that she respects her husband.

Genesis 2:22 And the Lord God [a]fashioned into a woman the rib which He had taken from the man, and brought her to the man.

Proverbs 18:22 He who finds a wife finds a good thing and obtains favor from the Lord.

1 Corinthians 7:2-5 [2] But because of sexual immoralities, each man is to have his own wife, and each woman is to have her own husband. [3] The husband must fulfill his duty to his wife, and likewise the wife also to her husband. [4] The wife does not have authority over her own body, but the husband does; and likewise, the husband also does not have authority over his own body, but the wife does. [5] [a] Stop depriving one another, except by agreement for a time so that you may devote yourselves to prayer, and [b]come together again so that Satan will not tempt you because of your lack of self-control.

1 Timothy 5:14 [14] Therefore, I want younger widows to get married, have children, manage their households, and give the enemy no opportunity for reproach.

1 Peter 3:1-2 [3] In the same way, you wives, be subject to your own husbands so that even if any of them are disobedient to the word, they may be won over without a word by the behavior of their wives, [2] as they observe your pure [a]and respectful behavior.

Genesis 1:27-28 [27] So God created man in His own image, in the image of God He created him; male and female He created them. [28] God blessed them; and God said to them, "Be fruitful and multiply, and fill the earth, and subdue it; and rule over the fish of the sea and over the birds of the sky and over every living thing that [a] moves on the earth."

Jeremiah 29:6 [6] Take wives and father sons and daughters, and take wives for your sons and give your daughters to husbands, so that they may give birth to sons and daughters; and grow in numbers there and do not decrease.

Hosea 2:19-20 I will betroth you to Me forever; Yes, I will betroth you to Me in righteousness and in justice, In favor and in compassion, 20 And I will betroth you to Me in faithfulness. Then you will know the Lord.

Hebrews 13:4 [4] Marriage is to be held in honor among all, and the marriage bed is to be undefiled; for God will judge the sexually immoral and adulterers.

2 Corinthians 6:14-16 [14] Do not be [a]mismatched with unbelievers; for what do righteousness and lawlessness share together, or what does light have in common with darkness? [15] Or what harmony does Christ have with [b]Belial, or [c]what does a believer share with an unbeliever? [16] Or what agreement does [d]the temple of God have with idols? For we are [e]the temple of the living God; just as God said,

"I will dwell among them and walk among them; And I will be their God, and they shall be My people.

Matthew 22:37-39 37 And He said to him, "'You shall love the Lord your God with all your heart, and with all your soul, and with all your mind.' 38 This is the great and [a]foremost commandment. 39 The second is like it, 'You shall love your neighbor as yourself.'

Hebrews 10:24 24 and let's consider how to [a]encourage one another in love and good deeds,

1 Corinthians 13:1-8 If I speak with the tongues of mankind and of angels, but do not have love, I have become a noisy gong or a clanging cymbal. 2 If I have the gift of prophecy and know all mysteries and all knowledge, and if I have all faith so as to remove mountains, but do not have love, I am nothing. 3 And if I give away all my possessions to charity, and if I surrender my body so that I may [a]glory, but do not have love, it does me no good.

4 Love is patient, love is kind, it is not jealous; love does not brag, it is not arrogant. 5 It does not act disgracefully, it does not seek its own benefit; it is not provoked, does not keep an account of a wrong suffered, 6 it does not rejoice in unrighteousness, but rejoices with the truth; 7 it [b]keeps every confidence, it believes all things, hopes all things, endures all things. 8 Love never fails;

FAMILY

Exodus 20:12 "Honor your father and your mother, so that you may live long in the land the LORD your God is giving you.

Psalm 127:3-5 Children are a heritage from the LORD, offspring a reward from him. [4] Like arrows in the hands of a warrior are children born in one's youth. [5] Blessed is the man whose quiver is full of them. They will not be put to shame when they contend with their opponents in court.

1 Corinthians 13:4-7 [4] Love is patient, love is kind. It does not envy, it does not boast, it is not proud. [5] It does not dishonor others, it is not self-seeking, it is not easily angered, it keeps no record of wrongs. [6] Love does not delight in evil but rejoices with the truth [7] It always protects, always trusts, always hopes, always perseveres.

1 Corinthians 11:3 But I want you to realize that the head of every man is Christ, and the head of the woman is man, and the head of Christ is God.

Colossians 3:20 Children, obey your parents in everything, for this pleases the Lord.

Psalm 27:10 Though my father and mother forsake me, the LORD will receive me.

1 Timothy 3:4-5 He must manage his own family well and see that his children obey him, and he must do so in a manner worthy of full respect. (If anyone does not know how to manage his own family, how can he take care of God's church?)

1 Timothy 5:8 Anyone who does not provide for their relatives, and especially for their own household, has denied the faith and is worse than an unbeliever.

Acts 10:2 He and all his family were devout and God-fearing; he gave generously to those in need and prayed to God regularly.

Colossians 3:13 Bear with each other and forgive one another if any of you has a grievance against someone. Forgive as the Lord forgave you.

Colossians 3:19 Husbands, love your wives and do not be harsh with them.

Ephesians 6:4 Fathers, do not exasperate your children; instead, bring them up in the training and instruction of the Lord.

Ephesians 5:33 However, each one of you also must love his wife as he loves himself, and the wife must respect her husband.

Ephesians 4:29-32 29 Watch your talk! No bad words should be coming from your mouth. Say what is good. Your words should help others grow as Christians. 30 Do not make God's Holy Spirit have sorrow for the way you live. The Holy Spirit has put a mark on you for the day you will be set free. 31 Put out of your life all these things: bad feelings about other people, anger, temper, loud talk, bad talk which hurts other people, and bad feelings which hurt other people. 32 You must be kind to each other. Think of the other person. Forgive other people just as God forgave you because of Christ's death on the cross.

Deuteronomy 6:6-9 6 Keep these words in your heart that I am telling you today. 7 Do your best to teach them to your children. Talk about them when you sit in your house and when you walk on the road and when you lie down and when you get up. 8 Tie them as something special to see on your hand and on your forehead. 9 Write them beside the door of your house and on your gates.

Proverbs 17:6, 17, 25 6 Grandchildren are the pride and joy of old men and a son is proud of his father. ... 17 A friend loves at all times. A brother is born to share troubles. 25 A foolish son is a sorrow to his father, and trouble to her who gave birth to him.

Proverbs 23:24-25 4 The father of a good child is very happy; parents who have wise children are glad because of them. 25 Make your father and mother happy; give your mother a reason to be glad.

Philippians 2:14-15 [14] Do everything without complaining or arguing. [15] Then you will be innocent and without any wrong. You will be God's children without fault. But you are living with crooked and mean people all around you, among whom you shine like stars in the dark world.

Romans 12:10-13 [10] Love each other like brothers and sisters. Give each other more honor than you want for yourselves. [11] Do not be lazy but work hard, serving the Lord with all your heart. [12] Be joyful because you have hope. Be patient when trouble comes, and pray at all times. [13] Share with God's people who need help. Bring strangers in need into your homes.

Proverbs 12:4 A wife of noble character is her husband's crown, but a disgraceful wife is like decay in his bones.

Ephesians 3:14-15 For this reason I kneel before the Father, **15** from whom every family in heaven and on earth derives its name.

Proverbs 15:27 The greedy bring ruin to their households, but the one who hates bribes will live.

Proverbs 31:15-17 She gets up while it is still night; she provides food for her family and portions for her female servants. [16] She considers a field and buys it; out of her earnings she plants a vineyard. [17] She sets about her work vigorously; her arms are strong for her tasks.

GROWING SPIRITUALLY

2 Peter 1:5-8 [5]Now for this very reason also, applying all diligence, in your faith supply moral [a]excellence, and in your moral excellence, knowledge, [6]and in your knowledge, self-control, and in your self-control, perseverance, and in your perseverance, godliness, [7]and in your godliness, brotherly kindness, and in your brotherly kindness, love. [8]For if these qualities are yours and are increasing, they do not make you useless nor unproductive in the true knowledge of our Lord Jesus Christ.

Hebrews 6:1 Therefore leaving the [a]elementary teaching about the [b]Christ, let us press on to [c]maturity, not laying again a foundation of repentance from dead works and of faith toward God,

1 Peter 2:2-3 [2]and like newborn babies, long for the [a]pure [b]milk of the word, so that by it you may grow [c]in respect to salvation, [3]if you have tasted [d]the kindness of the Lord.

2 Timothy 2:15 [15]Be diligent to present yourself approved to God as a worker who [a]does not need to be ashamed, accurately handling the word of truth.

Ephesians 3:14-19 [14]For this reason I bend my knees before the Father, [15]from whom [a]every family in heaven and on earth derives its name, [16]that He would grant you, according to the riches of His glory, to be strengthened with power through His Spirit in the inner [b]self, [17]so that Christ may dwell in your hearts through faith; and that you, being rooted and grounded in love, [18]may be able to comprehend with all the [c]saints what is the width and length and height and depth, [19]and to know the love of Christ which surpasses knowledge, that you may be filled to all the fullness of God.

1 Timothy 4:13-15 [13]Until I come, give your attention to the public [a]reading, to exhortation, and teaching. [14]Do not neglect the spiritual gift within you, which was granted to you through words of prophecy with the laying on of hands by the [b]council of elders. [15]Take pains with these things; be absorbed in them, so that your progress will be evident to all.

Colossians 1:9-11 ⁹For this reason we also, since the day we heard about it, have not ceased praying for you and asking that you may be filled with the [a]knowledge of His will in all spiritual wisdom and understanding, ¹⁰so that you will walk in a manner worthy of the Lord, [b]to please Him in all respects, bearing fruit in every good work and [c]increasing in the [d]knowledge of God; ¹¹strengthened with all power, according to [e]His glorious might, [f]for the attaining of all perseverance and [g]patience; joyously ¹²giving thanks to the Father, who has qualified us [h]to share in the inheritance of the [i]saints in light.

Colossians 3:16 ¹⁶Let the word of [a]Christ richly dwell within you, [b]with all wisdom teaching and admonishing [c]one another with psalms, hymns, and spiritual songs, singing with thankfulness in your hearts to God.

2 Corinthians 3:18 ¹⁸But we all, with unveiled faces, looking as in a mirror at the glory of the Lord, are being transformed into the same image from glory to glory, just as from the Lord, the Spirit.

Psalm 92:13 Planted in the house of the Lord, They will flourish in the courtyards of our God.

Philippians 1:6, 9-10 ⁶For I am confident of this very thing, that He who began a good work [a]among you will complete it [b]by the day of Christ Jesus. … ⁹And this I pray, that your love may overflow still more and more in real knowledge and all discernment, ¹⁰so that you may [g]discover the things that are excellent, that you may be sincere and blameless for the day of Christ;

Ephesians 4:14-16 ¹⁴[a]As a result, we are no longer to be children, tossed here and there by waves and carried about by every wind of doctrine, by the trickery of people, by craftiness [b]in deceitful scheming; ¹⁵but [c]speaking the truth in love, [d]we are to grow up in all aspects into Him who is the head, that is, Christ, ¹⁶from whom the whole body, being fitted and held together [e]by what every joint supplies, according to the [f]proper working of each individual

part, causes the growth of the body for the building up of itself in
love.

CHANGING THE WORLD

Matthew 5:14-16 [14] "You are the light of the world. A city set on a [a]hill cannot be hidden; [15] nor do people light a lamp and put it under a [b]basket, but on the lampstand, and it gives light to all who are in the house. [16] Your light must shine before people in such a way that they may see your good works and glorify your Father who is in heaven.

Daniel 12:3 [3] And [a]those who have insight will shine like the glow of the [b]expanse of heaven, and those who [c]lead the many to righteousness, like the stars forever and ever.

Mark 16:15-20 [15] And He said to them, "Go into all the world and preach the gospel to all creation. [16] The one who has believed and has been baptized will be saved; but the one who has not believed will be condemned. [17] These signs will accompany those who have believed: in My name they will cast out demons, they will speak with new tongues; [18] they will pick up serpents, and if they drink any deadly poison, it will not harm them; they will lay hands on the sick, and they will recover."

[19] So then, when the Lord Jesus had spoken to them, He was received up into heaven and sat down at the right hand of God. [20] And they went out and preached everywhere, while the Lord worked with them, and confirmed the word by the signs that followed.]]

Acts 1:8 [8] but you will receive power when the Holy Spirit has come upon you; and you shall be My witnesses both in Jerusalem and in all Judea, and Samaria, and as far as the remotest part of the earth."

Luke 4:18 "The Spirit of the Lord is upon Me, Because He anointed Me to bring good news to the poor. He has sent Me to proclaim release to captives, And recovery of sight to the blind, To set free those who are oppressed,

John 14:12 [12] Truly, truly I say to you, the one who believes in Me, the works that I do, he will do also; and greater works than these he will do, because I am going to the Father.

John 13:34-35 ³⁴ I am giving you a new commandment, that you love one another; just as I have loved you, that you also love one another. ³⁵ By this all people will know that you are My disciples: if you have love for one another."

1 John 5:3-5 ³ For this is the love of God, that we keep His commandments; and His commandments are not burdensome. ⁴ For [a]whoever has been born of God overcomes the world; and this is the victory that has overcome the world: our faith. ⁵ Who is the one who overcomes the world, but the one who believes that Jesus is the Son of God?

Hebrews 11:1-3, 32-34 Now faith is the certainty of things [a]hoped for, a [b]proof of things not seen. ²For by it the people of old [c] gained approval.

John 3:16 ¹⁶ "For God so loved the world, that He gave His only Son, so that everyone who believes in Him will not perish but have eternal life.

³ By faith we understand that the [d]world has been created by the word of God so that what is seen has not been made out of things that are visible. … ³²And what more shall I say? For time will fail me if I tell of Gideon, Barak, Samson, Jephthah, of David and Samuel and the prophets, ³³who by faith conquered kingdoms, performed acts of righteousness, obtained promises, shut the mouths of lions, ³² quenched the power of fire, escaped the edge of the sword, from weakness were made strong, became mighty in war, put foreign armies to flight.

Galatians 5:22-23 ²² But the fruit of the Spirit is love, joy, peace, patience, kindness, goodness, faithfulness, ²³ gentleness, self-control; against such things there is no law.

Galatians 5:14 ¹⁴ For the whole Law is fulfilled in one word, in the statement, "You shall love your neighbor as yourself."

Romans 12:2 ² And do not be conformed to this [a]world, but be transformed by the renewing of your mind, so that you may [b]prove what the will of God is, that which is good and [c]acceptable and perfect.

Colossians 3:23-24 23 Whatever you do, do your work [a]heartily, as for the Lord and not for people, 24 knowing that it is from the Lord that you will receive the reward [b]of the inheritance. It is the Lord Christ whom you serve.

1 Peter 2:9-12 9 But you are a chosen people, a royal priesthood, a holy nation, a people for *God's* own possession, so that you may proclaim the excellencies of Him who has called you out of darkness into His marvelous light; 10 for you once were not a people, but now you are the people of God; you had not received mercy, but now you have received mercy.

11 Beloved, I urge you as foreigners and strangers to abstain from fleshly lusts, which wage war against the soul. 12 Keep your behavior excellent among the Gentiles, so that in the thing in which they slander you as evildoers, they may [a]because of your good deeds, as they observe them, glorify God on the day of [b]visitation.

Romans 10:14 14 How then are they to call on Him in whom they have not believed? How are they to believe in Him whom they have not heard? And how are they to hear without a preacher?

John 15:12-13 12 "This is My commandment, that you love one another, just as I have loved you. 13 Greater love has no one than this, that a person will lay down his life for his friends.

John 6:44 44 No one can come to Me unless the Father who sent Me draws him; and I will raise him up on the last day.

Acts 4:31 31 And when they had prayed, the place where they had gathered together was shaken, and they were all filled with the Holy Spirit and began to speak the word of God with boldness.

John 4:13-14 13 Jesus answered and said to her, "Everyone who drinks of this water will be thirsty again; 14 but whoever drinks of the water that I will give him shall never be thirsty; but the water that I will give him will become in him a fountain of water springing up to eternal life.

HOW GOD CAN HELP YOUR BUSINESS

Exodus 35:35 He has filled them with skill to do every sort of work done by an engraver or by a designer or by an embroiderer in blue and purple and scarlet yarns and fine twined linen, or by a weaver— by any sort of workman or skilled designer.

Leviticus 19:13 You shall not oppress your neighbor or rob him. The wages of a hired worker shall not remain with you all night until the morning.

Deuteronomy 25:13 You shall not have in your bag two kinds of weights, a large and a small. You shall not have in your house two kinds of measures, a large and a small. A full and fair weight you shall have, a full and fair measure you shall have, that your days may be long in the land that the LORD your God is giving you.

Psalm 112:5 It is well with the man who deals generously and lends, who conducts his affairs with justice.

Proverbs 11:1 A false balance is an abomination to the LORD, but a just weight is his delight

Proverbs 22:16 Whoever oppresses the poor to increase his own wealth, or gives to the rich, will only come to poverty.

Jeremiah 22:13 Woe to him who builds his house by unrighteousness, and his upper rooms by injustice, who makes his neighbor serve him for nothing and does not give him his wages.

Job 31:13 If I have rejected the cause of my manservant or my maidservant, when they brought a complaint against me, what then shall I do when God rises up? When he makes inquiry, what shall I answer him?

James 5:4 Behold, the wages of the laborers who mowed your fields, which you kept back by fraud, are crying out against you, and the cries of the harvesters have reached the ears of the Lord of hosts.

Exodus 31:3-5 And I have filled him with the Spirit of God, with ability and intelligence, with knowledge and all craftsmanship, to devise artistic designs, to work in gold, silver, and bronze, in cutting stones for setting, and in carving wood, to work in every craft.

Exodus 35:10 All who are skilled among you are to come and make everything the LORD has commanded.

Proverbs 22:29 Do you see a man skillful in his work? He will stand before kings; he will not stand before obscure men."

1 Corinthians 12:4-6 Now there are varieties of gifts, but the same Spirit; and there are varieties of service, but the same Lord; and there are varieties of activities, but it is the same God who empowers them all in everyone.

Ephesians 2:10 For we are God's handiwork, created in Christ Jesus to do good works, which God prepared in advance for us to do.

1 Peter 4:10-11 As each has received a gift, use it to serve one another, as good stewards of God's varied grace: whoever speaks, as one who speaks oracles of God; whoever serves, as one who serves by the strength that God supplies—in order that in everything God may be glorified through Jesus Christ. To him belong glory and dominion forever and ever.

Proverbs 13:11 Wealth gained hastily will dwindle, but whoever gathers little by little will increase it.

Proverbs 14:23 In all toil there is profit, but mere talk tends only to poverty.

Proverbs 15:16 Better is a little with the fear of the LORD than great treasure and trouble with it.

Proverbs 16:8 Better is a little with righteousness than great revenues with injustice.

Proverbs 21:5 The plans of the diligent lead surely to abundance, but everyone who is hasty comes only to poverty. Better is a poor man who walks in his integrity than a rich man who is crooked in his ways

Proverbs 28:6 Whoever works his land will have plenty of bread, but he who follows worthless pursuits will have plenty of poverty.

Colossians 3:17 And whatever you do, in word or deed, do everything in the name of the Lord Jesus, giving thanks to God the Father through him.

Colossians 3:23 Whatever you do, work heartily, as for the Lord and not for men, knowing that from the Lord you will receive the inheritance as your reward. You are serving the Lord Christ.

Luke 16:10 One who is faithful in a very little is also faithful in much, and one who is dishonest in a very little is also dishonest in much.

Deuteronomy 8:18 You shall remember the LORD your God, for it is he who gives you power to get wealth, that he may confirm his covenant that he swore to your fathers, as it is this day.